NEW STOCK TREND DETECTOR

A REVIEW OF THE 1929-1932 PANIC
AND THE 1932-1935 BULL MARKET

With New Rules for Detecting Trends of Stocks

WILLIAM D. GANN

FOREWARD

A man writes the best and does the most good for others when his object in or writing is not to make money or gratify ambition or gain publicity, but to help others who need help and appreciate his efforts.

When I wrote TRUTH OF THE STOCK TAPE in 1923, it was because there was a demand for a book of that kind. People needed the help that I could give them and the benefit of my experience and knowledge. In that book I gave the best I had and received my reward. People appreciated my efforts. They bought the book then and they are still buying it. They say it is a good book and more than worth the money. That is very gratifying to me.

After the 1929 bull market culminated, there was a demand for a new book to meet changed conditions under the so-called "New Era," so I wrote WALL STREET STOCK SELECTOR in the spring of 1930. I gave freely of my knowledge and benefit of years of experience. This book helped others to protect their principle and make profits. People who read the book pronounced it one of the best. It is still selling, and again I have been rewarded.

No man can learn all there is to know about forecasting the trend of stocks in 3, 5, 10, or 20 years but if he is a deep student and hard worker, he learns more and knowledge comes easier after years of experience. I knew more about determining the trend of stocks in 1923 than I did in 1911. Seven more years of experience gave me more knowledge and enabled me to write THE WALL STREET STOCK SELECTOR in 1939 and give my readers the benefit of my increased knowledge. Now, after five more years have elapsed my experience and practical test of new rules have enabled me to learn more of value since 1930. The 1929-1932 panic and what has followed since, gave me valuable experience and I have gained more knowledge about detecting the right stocks to buy and sell. I cannot lose if I pass this knowledge on to those who will appreciate it.

Hundreds of people who have read my books have asked me to write a new book. Again, I answer the call and meet the popular demand with NEW STOCK TREND DETECTOR. I believe the book will help others to avoid some of the pitfalls of reckless speculation. If I can lead a few more to the field of knowledge, I shall again be amply repaid for my efforts.

W.D. Gann
33 Wall Street, New York

CONTENTS

CHAPTER I

A NEW DEAL IN WALL STREET

Since writing TRUTH OF THE STOCK TAPES in 1923 and WALL STREET STOCK SELECTOR in 1936, the greatest panic that the world has ever seen has taken place, culminating with the greatest stock decline in history, reaching extreme low levels on July 8, 1932. Conditions have changed since 1929 and new laws have passed effecting stock market movements. The passing of the law supervising stock exchanges has made a great change in the action of the stock market and made it necessary to formulate new rules to meet the changed conditions. The Bible says, "Old things pass away and new ones come to take their places." "A wise man changes his mind, a fool never." The man who refuses to change when conditions change, or to see the new way of doing things is doomed to failure.

This is an age of progress. We move forward, not backward. We cannot stand still. We must go ahead with progress or retrograde into the list of the "has beens." Henry Ford made hundreds of millions of dollars with the old Model "T" car. It was a good car in its day and Ford was satisfied with it, but time and conditions changed. The public changed and demanded an up-to- date, better car. Henry Ford, being a wise man, saw the "handwriting on the wall" and changed his mind. In the midst of the world's greatest depression, Ford closed his factory and over $100,000,000 to develop a new and better car, or as the boys say, "He made a lady out of 'Lizzie.'" He was not actuated by the desire for more money when he developed this new car. It was pride and ambition and not greed that urged him to keep the public's good will by giving them a better car at a lower price. The public responded quickly and the new Ford became a leader. Each year Ford has improved his car until the 1936 Model is the best car yet produced.

Politician with selfish motives have always preached against Wall Street and misled the public in regard to the way business is handled on the New York Stock Exchange and the type of men who handle it. There is no business in the world where a higher type of honor exists than among the men who are members of the New York Stock Exchange. No businessmen in the world live up to their contracts like the brokers on the floor of the New York Stock Exchange. In other lines of business, contracts are made for future delivery of different classes of goods, lumber, textiles and mercantile products of various kinds. In cases of this kind, when prices advance, the buyer calls on the seller to make delivery of the products, but when prices decline he cancels his contract and leaves the seller to get out the best way he can. I quote from a letter from a prominent lumberman:

"In marketing lumber, it is impossible to profit from future price changes even if one should be fortunate enough to anticipate them, for the reason the purchaser may cancel the contract if prices decline, but the sawmill is expected to fill the contract at the sale prices even if prices advance above it. With few exceptions, this is the general rule covering sales by sawmills to factories that consume the major part of hardwood lumber in the United States. In the decline of the lumber market the first part of 1934, my company had lumber orders cancelled, amounting to 1, 400,000 feet. I know this must seem strange to you, having operated so long where all contracts are made binding on both buyer and seller.

"I have a high regard for the business methods used in Wall Street. After trading there 10 years, it is my opinion there is probably no place or business so free of repudiations or acts of dishonesty."

Such a thing as a member of the New York Stock Exchange ever attempting to cancel his contract for a stock he buys or sells is unheard of. When a broker buys or sells stocks on the New York Stock Exchange by raising his hand or nodding his head, he is bound by his honor to live up to the contract and he does. No matter how much the stock goes against him or what the loss is, he never welches. He does not attempt to cancel his contract. He makes his delivery. The brokers and the managers of the New York Stock Exchange are honest and reliable men. The public has been confused as to the position of the New York Stock Exchange, which is but the means and the machinery

7

for carrying on transactions between buyer and seller. The brokers on the floor of the New York Stock Exchange are in no way responsible for the actions of pools or outside deals, which at times have been handled by unscrupulous manipulators in the past, but the public has been led to believe that the Stock Exchange and its members were working against them. The brokers simply buy and sell for a commission and give the best service possible to their customers. The New York Stock Exchange serves a useful purpose. The greater part of the manufacturers of this country have their stock listed on the New York Stock Exchange and every buyer and seller can know every day what the prices are. Without the New York Stock Exchange there would be no Clearing House, no place where people who need money could instantly turn their securities into cash. The fact that the New York Stock Exchange has been in existence since 1792 proves that it fills an economic need, or it would have long since been out of business.

For years, Wall Street and the New York Stock Exchange and its rules and way of doing business were considered the best and needed no changes. Then came the "New Deal" and the Securities Exchange Law which compelled changes in rules. Before these laws were put into effect, the New York Stock Exchange saw the need of a new way of doing business and keeping the public thoroughly informed of the way business was carried on.

WHY BLAME WALL STREET AND THE NEW YORK STOCK EXCHANGE?

The man who makes profits never gives credit to Wall Street brokers or any one else for his profits. He takes credit for making them himself. Then, why should he blame his losses on someone else?

If you make a trade in stocks and lose money, do not let politicians lead you to believe that pool managers, manipulators, or the New York Stock Exchange are the cause of your losing money, because they are not. No one forces you to make a trade. You buy or sell stocks because you hope to make profits, and you would not kick if you made them; therefore, don't play the "baby act" and blame someone if you lose. If you had carelessly run in front of an automobile and were injured, would you blame the automobile or the driver for your carelessness? Just because people have been killed by cars is no reason why laws should be passed to keep automobiles off the roads and streets. Politicians have tried to pass laws for years to restrict the useful operations of the Stock Exchange and Commodity Exchanges just because people who have lost money have complained to Congressmen against the Exchanges which serve a useful purpose.

THE LAW OF SUPPLY AND DEMAND

The prices on the New York Stock Exchange, the New York Cotton Exchange and the Chicago Board of Trade are governed by Supply and Demand. No matter whether the buying or selling is by the public, by pools, or by manipulators, prices decline when there are more sellers than buyers and prices advance when stocks are scarce and when there are more buyers than sellers. The members of these Exchanges do not make the markets; they only do the buying and selling for the public and large operators. The pools and large operators in the past have manipulated prices, but no blame should be placed on the Exchanges which merely act as a clearing house for the transactions.

If you could find out the rules the master market makers use to make money, you would buy and sell when they do and make profits, wouldn't you? If you knew what the big operations were doing, you certainly would follow them. People often ask me: "How can I make some easy money?" or "How can I make some money quick?" There is no way to make easy money, and there is no way to make money quickly until you have acquired knowledge yourself. You must pay for whatever you get. What is worth having is worth paying for. Getting money quick and easy does more harm than good.

You can learn what the big operators are doing by being a good Wall Street detective. You can detect what the "powers that be" are doing, by a study of Supply and Demand. The record of the total sales and the high and low prices of every stock are published daily in the newspapers throughout the country. There is no secret about it. It is just up to you to follow rules. If you study Supply and Demand and follow my rules, you can detect the trend and make money.

HOW NEW DEAL HAS CHANGED CONDITIONS

The New Deal in Washington and the laws passed have changed stock trading so far as the public is concerned. Washed sales under the Securities Exchange Law are no longer permitted. The specialist is restricted on tracks that he can make for himself. Short selling has been curtailed. A heavy increase in the amount of margin required to carry stocks has reduced the volume of trading. Taxes have been increased, both income taxes and other taxes, which causes traders and investors to hold on longer and not sell out their stocks because they would have to pay such a large amount of their profits to the Government. This changes the technical position of the market; makes it stronger at times but eventually will make it much weaker and stocks will decline much faster because the short interest in the future will be limited, pool operations will be smaller, and the support in the market by the specialists will be much smaller than it has been in the past.

There will come a time when the market will run into a real heavy selling: bids and offers will be far apart. It will be hard to sell stocks when everybody wants to sell and nobody wants to buy. Another thing, heavy margins will work against the market and cause a greater decline, because when people put up 40 to 60% margin, they will hold out longer, or until the margin is nearly exhausted, then everybody will want to sell at the same time and there will be few buyers. It is my opinion that the laws past to regulate the Stock Exchange will not prove beneficial to the public in the future, just as many laws already passed by the Administration under President Roosevelt have already proved to be detrimental and the Supreme Court has found it necessary to declare them unconstitutional.

CHAPTER II

FOUNDATION FOR SUCCESSFUL TRADING

"Wisdom is the principle thing; therefore get wisdom: and with all thy getting get understanding": PROVERBS 4:7

Have you ever stopped to think and make a careful analysis why you have lost money in stocks or why you have been wrong when you made a trade? If you have, you have probably found that you traded on hope, bankers' opinions, or relied on tips, or you guessed yourself. Another reason, because you did not admit to yourself that you could be wrong and did not protect yourself when you made the trade. But regardless of how you made the mistake and had the loss, the fault was your own, because you had no definite rules or plan or way to know just when to buy or sell.

You should learn to trade on knowledge, which will eliminate fear and hope. Then, when hope and fear no longer influence you, knowledge will give you nerve to trade and make profits. You should learn the truth about a stock, then learn to how apply all the rules that I have given in my books TRUTH OF THE STOCK TAPE, WALL STREET STOCK SELECTOR and in this book, NEW STOCK TREND DETECTOR. Then you will have a knowledge of trading and an education that you never had before, and when you make a trade, it will be for a good and sufficient reason and on definite rules. You will neither hope nor fear then. You will trade on fact. You will protect your capital and profits by the use of stop loss orders and will make profits.

There is one way to always correct a mistake if you buy or sell a stock against the trend, and that is to place a *stop loss order*. A stop loss order protects you in many ways. When you buy a stock, place a stop loss order 1, 2, or 3 points away. Then if you are out of town or out of reach of your broker, and then some sudden, unexpected event happens to cause a sharp decline and the stock reaches your stop loss order, you are automatically sold out. The stock might go to points lower the same day before they could reach you. Yet, you are protected because you had your order with the broker to sell. You did not have to be there to watch it and did not have to be where the broker could reach you.

There is nothing that will give you more valuable information or enable you to tell more what a stock is going to do than to study its past actions and apply the rules that I give in my books. If you know what a stock has done in the past, it will help you to determine what it will do in the future. All of the buying and selling is recorded and registered in the price of the stocks, which is influenced by Supply and Demand. Price movement, if studied correctly, will tell you more about the stock than brokers can tell you, or newspapers or any other kind of so-called "inside" information.

LEARN TO BE INDEPENDENT

The greatest help that one man can give another is to show him how to help himself. The man or woman who depends on others for advice, for inside information or for what others think about the stock market, will never make a success of speculation or anything else. You must learn to be independent. Learn to do by doing and to know by study and application. Then you will have confidence and courage that no one else can give you.

An intelligent man will not follow blindly the opinion of others without knowing what their opinion is based on, but when he himself sees, understands and knows the rules that forecast stock market trends, then he becomes a good Wall Street detective. He detects the future trends and follows them with confidence. He no longer says, "If I knew the information I get on Chrysler was right, I would buy 500 shares instead of 100." When he sees and understands why Chrysler gives a definite indication of advance, he then has no fear and no hope, but has confidence and courage to buy 500 shares.

No matter what business you are interested in, learn all you can about it. The most important thing, outside of your health to protect is your money. Therefore take time to study and prepare yourself to handle your money yourself and do not depend forever and entirely upon others.

A DEFINITE PLAN

Make up your mind now to have a definite plan or aim in the future. Decide to follow rules when you buy or sell stocks, but first prove to yourself that the rules are good and that they will work.

The rules given in my books are good practical rules. You can prove them to your own satisfaction in a short period of time. Many men and women who have bought my books, TRUTH OF THE STOCK TAPE and WALL STREET STOCK SELECTOR, have learned the rules, followed them and made a success, and you can do the same if you work and study hard.

I have studied and improved my Methods every year for the past 35 years. I am still learning. Some of my greatest discoveries were made between 1932 and 1935. After long years of study and research, I have simplified and made my rules practical so that others can apply them as easily as I can. I have eliminated unnecessary details; have cut down the work so you can get results quicker; and have made profits by following strictly the same rules.

KNOWLEDGE BRINGS SUCCESS

The door that opens to big profits has but one key to unlock it and that key is Knowledge. You cannot get that knowledge without work. I have made a success by hard work and you, too, can make plenty of money out of the stock market if you study and work hard enough. Work is the way to find the Royal Road to riches in Wall Street.

When the Queen of Sheba visited King Solomon, she did not go for his bankroll or jewelry. It was his wisdom that she sought, and his great wisdom her love, so Arthur Brisbane says, and I have great respect for Mr. Brisbane's opinion. If you get practical knowledge on stocks and commodities you will have no trouble in getting capital to make more money with. Money always comes to knowledge; without knowledge money is worthless. You can increase your money and make wise investments when you acquired knowledge.

QUALIFICATIONS FOR SUCCESS

1ST: KNOWLEDGE

First and most important: You must get Knowledge.

Make up your mind to spend thirty minutes to one hour per day studying stock market movements for the next five years. Then you will get knowledge of how to detect market trends and will make money. You will not be looking for a quick and easy way to make money. You will have paid in advance with time and study. The more time you put into getting knowledge, the more money you will make later.

2ND: PATIENCE

This is one of the very important qualifications for success. When you buy or sell you must have the patience to wait for opportunities to get in right. Then, you must have the patience to wait until there is a change in trend before you close a trade or take profits.

3RD: NERVE

I can give a man the best gun in the world and if he hasn't the nerve to pull the trigger, he will never kill any game. You can have all the knowledge in the world and if you haven't the knowledge to buy or sell, you cannot make any money, but Knowledge does give a man nerve; makes him bold and enables him to act at the right time.

4TH: GOOD HEALTH

After you have gained knowledge, acquired patience and developed nerve, the next important quality is good health. No man can have patience and nerve and do his best unless his health is good. If you are in bad health, you become despondent, you lose hope, you have too much fear, and you will be unable to act. I have been through the game for all these years; have tried to trade when I have been in bad health and have seen others try to trade, but I never saw a man yet make a

14

success speculating when his health was bad. The thing to do if your health gets bad is to quit business, quit speculating and get your health back, for health is wealth.

5TH: CAPITAL

With all these qualifications for making a success, you must have capital, but if you have knowledge and patience, you can start with a small capital and make a lot of money, provided you use stop loss orders, take small losses, and do not overtrade.

Remember, never buck the trend: after you detect the trend, go with it regardless of what you think, hope or fear and you will make a success. Read and follow "Twenty-four Never-failing Rules" on page 18-19 of WALL STREET STOCK SELECTOR.

CHAPTER III

HISTORY REPEATS

Future stock market movements can be forecast by a study of past history and past movements. By knowing the time when the greatest advances have taken place and the times when the greatest panics and declines have occurred and the time periods to watch for major and minor changes in trend, you can detect what to expect in the future. Just remember one thing, whatever has happened in the past in stock market and Wall Street will happen again. Advances and bull markets will come in the future and panics will come in the future, just as they have in the past. This is the working out of a natural law and the balancing of time with price. It is action in one direction and reaction in the opposite direction. In order to make profits, you must learn to follow the trend and change when the trend changes.

War in the past has always had a great affect upon stocks and commodity prices. The starting of wars often has produced panics or sharp declines followed by booms, and after the war was over, there was another sharp decline or a panic, followed by another boom with probably higher levels than occurred during the war days. It is important, therefore, to study the action of stocks and commodities around the beginning of war periods and after the ending of wars in order to detect what may happen in the future when these same conditions repeat.

It is important to study the time that has elapsed between bottoms and tops and the greatest duration of any bull campaign as well as the duration of any panic or decline.

W. D. GANN AVERAGES
1856-1874

1856 - If you will refer to my averages in WALL STREET STOCK SELECTOR, you will see that in February 1856, stocks reached a high of 95½. Then followed a period of distribution.

1857 - In January, the last high was reached at 92, from which a panicky decline started. This was the 1857 panic, which culminated in October 1857, with the Averages down 57 points in a period of six months.

1858 - A rally followed to March 1858, lasting five months.
1859 - The market declined and made low in June, down 15 months.

1860 - In September, the high was made again, 15 months up.

1861 - Last low on the Averages at 48 in March. Time of decline, 7 months, the last low before the Civil War boom. At this point watch the length of time period to compare with other war booms.

1864 - In April the Averages reached a high of 155. Time, 36 months from the last bottom and at no time did they decline more than two consecutive months.

1865 - March, low 88, down 67 points in 11 months; October, high 121; time, 7 months.

1866 - February, low 100; time, 4 months; October, high 125, 8 months from the low and 19 months from 1865 low.

1867 - April, low of reaction 104; time, 6 months. From this low the big after-war boom followed.

1869 - July, high 181; time, 27 months from April 1867; 50 months from March 1865 low, which was the most important time period to measure from, being 8 years and 3 months. The last stage of the boom lasted 27 months. This ended the great after-war boom, and a panic followed.

17

1873 - November, low 84, a decline of 96 points from the high of 1869. Time of bear campaign, 52 months, but from August 1870 to May 1871, there was a rally of 9 months and from January to June 1872, a rally of 6 months; and from November 1872 low, a rally to January 1873, a two months' rally, which indicated a weak market, just as we had in 1931 and 1932.

1874 - February, high 107. Time of the rally, 3 months. In June and October, lows were reached; time period, 4 months and 8 months. Then the rails rallied to May 1875.

12 INDUSTRIAL STOCK AVERAGES
1875-1896

Here we begin with 12 Industrial Stocks which were about the same as the Dow-Jones Averages, which started in 1897.

1875 - March, high 53; October, low 48.

1876 - February, high 52.

1877 - October, low 36, a decline of 16 months without much rally.

1879 - A real bull market began in August 1879 and lasted until June 1881, a period of 22 months.

1881 - June, high 72, an advance of 47 months with a 6- months' reaction in 1878 and 1879, and 2 to 3 months' reaction several times.

1881-1885:
From June 1881 to June 1884, there was an extreme bear campaign with the Averages down from 72 to 42. The Bear Campaign lasted 36 months with only a 2 months' rally, like the rally from July to September 1932. Then, from a top of a rally in August 1884, there was a decline to January 1885, making a double bottom at 42 against the low of June 1884.

1885 - November, high 57, up 10 months.

18

1886 - May, low of reaction at 53.

1887 - End of bull market in May; time, 34 months from 1884 low and 27 months from the secondary bottom of January 1885.

1888 - April, low of bear market at 51. Time, 11 to 12 months.

1889 - June and September highs at 63.

1890 - A third top at 63 was reached in January 1890, making this almost a triple top and selling level.

1888-1890 - The time from April 1888 to January 1890 was 21 months.

1890 - December, low of decline at 49. Time, 11 months from the last high of January 1890.

1893 - January, high of bull market at 72. Time, 25 months from 1890. Then followed the panic of 1893. August 1893, bottom of bear market at 40, down 32 points in 7 months.

1895 - High of the bull campaign in June at 58; time, 22 months. This was really a rally in a bull market, for the main trend was still down.

1896 - Bryn Silver Panic: August 1896, low of the Dow-Jones Averages at 29. Time, 14 months from the top of 1895, and 43 months from January 1893 top. After this panicky decline was over, the McKinley boom started, which started for several years.

DOW-JONES INDUSTRIAL AVERAGES
1897-1935

1897 - September, high 55. Time, 12 months.

1898 - March, low 42. Time, 6 months from the previous top.

1899 - April, high 78. Time, 13 months. A sharp decline followed in May; then a slow advance. September, high 78, same as the April high. Time, from 1896, 36 months and from March 1898, 18 months.

1900 - September, low 53. Time, 12 months. End of bear market.

1901 - June, high 78, same as top in 1899, a third top and the end of the bull market. December, low 62. Time, 6 months.

1902 - April, high 69. Time, 4 months.

1903 - October and November, low 42½. Time, 28 to 29 months from 1901 top; 8 months from top of last rally in February 1903. After 1903, the Industrial Averages became more active and were leaders, whereas previous to this time the railroads were the most active and leading stocks. The rails did lead from 1896 to 1906, which was the last high until 1924-1929 boom when the rails reached the highest in history. We will now continue with the Industrials.

1906 - January, high 103. Time, 27 months from 1903 low and never reacted more than 2 months, an indication of a strong bull market. Low of reaction at 86 in August. Time, 6 months. October, high 97.

1907 - January, high 97, from which a big decline started. March 14, 1907, a panicky decline known as the "silent panic." Stocks declined 20 points that day. Low of the Averages was 76. Rallied to 85 in May, then declined to 53 in November. Time, 22 months from January1906 high. Accumulation took place and a bull market started from November.

1909 - October, high 101, top of bull campaign. Time, 23 months. Never reacted more then 3 months.

1910 - July, low 73, bottom of decline. Time, 9 months.

1911- June, high 87. Time, 11 months. A sharp decline followed. September, low 73, same low as July 1910.

1912 - October, high 94, top of bull wave. Time, 13 months.

1913 - June, bottom at 53. Time, 8 months, the third time at the same level. This is very important and always indicates that an advance should follow as long as the third bottom is not broken. September, high 83. Time, 3 months. December, low 76.

1914 - March, high 83, same as September 1913. War was declared in Europe in the early part of July and the Stock Exchange closed at the end of July and remained closed until December 1914. After the exchange opened in December 1914, the Industrial Averages declined to 53 1/3, the same low level reached in 1907. Time from October 1912, 26 months.

1915 - December, high 99½, just under the top of 1909. Time, 12 months from 1914 low.

1916 - April, low 85. Time of reaction, 4 months. November, high 110, top of bull campaign. This was a new high level for the Dow-Jones Industrial Averages. Time, 23 months from December 1914.

1917 - February, low 87. June, high 99. Time, 4 months. Then a big panicky decline followed. December, low 66, bottom of bear campaign. Time, 13 months.

1919 - November, high 119½, top of bull campaign. Time, 23 months from December 1917 low. No reaction lasted more than 3 months.

1920 - December, low 66, same low as 1917. Time from top, 13 months.

1921 - May, high 79. August, low 64, not 3 points under the 1917 and 1920 lows, which was a sign of good support and indicated that a bull market would follow. Top from 1919 top, 21 months.

1921-1929 BULL CAMPAIGN

From the low in August 1921 followed the greatest bull market in the history of the United States, culminating in September 1929.

1923 - Top of first section of this great bull market was reached in March 1923, with the Averages at 105. Time, 19 months. Low of reaction at 86 in October. Time, 7 months.

1924 - February, high of rally, 105, from which a 3 months' reaction followed. May, low 89. May 1924 was the real beginning of the Coolidge Bull Market.

1925 - In January the Dow-Jones Averages crossed 120, the high of 1919, which indicated much higher prices because the volume of trading was heavy and stocks were very active.

1926 - February, high 162. Time from last low, 21 months. March, bottom of a sharp decline, the Averages declining to 136 and some stocks declining 100 points in this short period. The Averages held for a few months in a narrow trading range and then started up again. After that no reaction lasted more than 2 months until 1929.

1929 - On September 3, 1929, when final top was reached, the Industrial Averages made 386, up 322 points from the 1921 low and 300 points from the 1923 low. Time from 1921 low to 1929 high, 97 months. (Refer to 1851-1869 and you will see how this compares. The Bull Campaign at that time lasted 99 months, which was one of the greatest in history until 1929.) The time from the 1923 low to the 1929 high was 71 months, and from the 1924 low, 64 months; from March 1926 low, 42 months; and from the last low of October 1926, 35 months.

It is before and after wars that you can determine the greatest length of time a bull market may run and the greatest length of time a panicky decline may run. The culmination of the bull Market in September 1929 was really the result of a long-tend business cycle which began in August 1896 and continued for 33 years, with each campaign in market making higher prices, which showed that the long-trend was up. It was only natural that after the greatest bull market in history, the greatest bear market in history must follow, and to determine how long the bear campaign might run, you would look back to see what had happened after previous war booms!

1869-1873: From 1869-1873 we find that the time period was 53 months and that the market had a 9 months' rally, a 6 months' rally and a 2 months' rally during that period.

1871-1873: May 1871 top to November 1873 low. Time, 30 months.

1881-1884: Then we refer to 1881 to 1884, and find that the bear market lasted 36 months.

1893-1896: Then we refer to 1893 to August 1896 and find that the bear market lasted 43 months.

Going back over all the records, we find that the greatest bear market had lasted not more than 43 months and the smallest had been as short as 12 months. Some of them had culminated around 27 months, 30 months, 34 months, and in extreme declines, anywhere from 36 to 43 months.

Therefore, from 1929, based on past records, we would begin to watch for bottom around the 30th to 36th month and then again around the 40th to 43rd month.

1929-1932 BEAR MARKET

First Section of the Great Bear Market - September 3, 1929 to November 13, 1920.

The Dow-Jones 30 Industrial Averages declined from a high of 386 on September 3, 1929 to a low of 198 on November 13, 1920, a decline of 188 points in 71 days - the greatest decline in the history of the New York Stock Exchange in the shortest period of time.

A secondary rally culminated on April 17, 1930 with the Averages at 297, up 99 points in 155 days. The volume of sales decreased in April. The top of a secondary rally is always an important point to watch.

Second Section of the Great Bear Market - April 17, 1930 to December 17, 1930:

From the top on April 17, 1930 there was a decline to December 17, 1930.
The averages declined from 297 to 155, a decline of 142 points. Time, 244 days or 8 months.

The second rally carried prices to top on February 24, 1931, with the averages at 196, up 41 points in 69 days. This shorter time period and smaller number of points indicated weakness and showed main trend down.

Third Section of the Great Bear Market - February 24, 1931 to January 5, 1932:

After top in February 1931, a decline started and in April 1931 the Average broke the lows of December 1930. On June 2, 1931 declined to 120, the top of November 1919. My rule is that old tops become bottoms and old bottoms later become tops; therefore, from the old top level a rally could be expected. From June 2nd to June 27th the Averages advanced to 157½, up 37½ points in 25 days. This was a quick rally in a bear market and showed weakness since stocks could not rally one full month. After this rally there was a decline to October 5, 1931, with the Averages at 85½, down 72 points in 100 days. A quick rally followed to November 9, 1931, with the price at 119, up to the bottom of June 2, 1931. Here we would expect selling at the old bottom, according to my rule of old bottoms becoming tops. This was a rally of 35 points in 35 days. The main trend down was resumed and on December 17, 1931, just one year from the low of December 1930, the Averages reached 72; had a quick rally to 83 on December19th and declined to 70 on January 5, 1932, down 49½ from the last from the last high of November 9, 1931. The decline lasted 57 days, but was 192 days from June 27, 1931 and was really the end of the Third Section of the Great Bear Market because after the low of January 5, 1932, the market rallied to March 9, 1932. The Averages reached 89½, up 19½ points in 64 days, a very feeble rally for the time required, which showed that liquidation had not run its course.

Fourth Section of the Great Bear Market - March 9 to July 9, 1932:

The fourth and last section of the Great Bear Market lasted 4 months, from March 9, 1932 to July 8, 1932, or 121 days, a shorter period with a price decline of 49 points. Note that this was about the same number of points as the decline from November 9, 1931 to January 5, 1932. From March 9 to July 8, 1932, when the final wave of liquidation was taking place, the greatest rally on Averages was 7 points, and each decline from the small rallies got shorter and the volume of sales less, which showed that liquidation was about over. The last decline from June 16th to July 8th was 11 points. Then the Great Bear Market ended and the trend turned up.

On July 8, 1932, the Dow-Jones Averages made low at 40½, down 34 months from the 1929 top and 27 months from the April 1930 top, which were time periods when we would expect a sharp, panicky decline to end, especially a decline which had carried the Averages down 345 points in 34 months and wiped out the gains of 33 years in many stocks.

Note that in April 1897, the last low was 40½, from which the real bull market started, and in July 1932 the Averages reached this same level, 40½, although there was a different number of stocks

Previous to the bottom in July 1932, the volume of sales and time periods all indicated that the market was near the end of the bear campaign.

1932-1935 BULL MARKET

First Section of Bull Market - July 8 to September 8, 1932:

From the low of 40 ½ on July 8, 1932 the Dow-Jones 30 Industrial Averages rallied to 81 on September 8, 1932, and advance of 40 points in 62 days. This was a fast advance on short covering and some good buying, but when stocks could not hold and go higher in the third month, it was an indication of lower prices. The large volume also made it plain that this was only the first rally in the bull campaign, from which a secondary decline must follow.

25

Secondary Decline - Just as the Bear Market had a secondary rally from November 1929 to April 1930, so after the market had given a signal that the Bear Market was over, there was a secondary decline, which lasted until February 27, 1933, with the Averages at 49½, down 31 points from the top of September 8, 1932 in 172 days, but 9 points above the 1932 lows. At this time President Roosevelt was inaugurated and banks closed. The New York Stock Exchange closed for one week. The volume of sales was very small, which indicated liquidation was over. When news is the worst, it is time to buy stocks, as a Bull Market begins in gloom and ends in glory with nothing but good news.

Second Section of Bull Market - February 27, 1933 to July 17, 1933:

The averages advanced from the low at 29½ in February 1933 to a high of 110½ on July 17, 1933, up 61 days in 141 days. Time, 12 months from July 1932 low and 5 months from February 1933 low. My rule tells you to always watch for a change in trend one year, two years, etc., for any important top or bottom. The sales during May, June, and July were larger than at the end of the Bull Market in 1929. This enormous volume was an indication that the market was reaching a culmination and a sign of top.

A reaction followed. The Averages reached bottom at 82½ on October 21st, 1933, down 28 points in 96 days. The volume of sales was small. In view of that fact that the Averages declined only 2 points under the low point of July 29, 1933 and did not decline to the top of 81½ made on September 8, 1932, indicated that the main trend was still up.

Third Section of Bull Market - October 21, 1933 to February 5, 1934:

From the low of 82½ on October 21, 1933 the Averages worked up to 111½ on February 5, 1934, just one point above the top of July 17, 1933, a double top on large volume of 5 million shares per day. This was an advance of 29 points in 107 days. Time, 19 months from July 1932 low and four months from October 1933 low. Since the Averages failed to go thorough 112, the market indicated top.

Then there was a reaction to July 26, 1934, with the Averages declining to 84½, a decline of 27 points in 171 days, the length of time as the

26

reaction from September 8, 1932 to February 27, 1933. Time, from February 1934 top, 5 months. The volume of sales on July 26 was 3 million shares and the Averages were 2 points above the low of October 21, 1933. This large volume and higher support level was an indication of bottom.

Fourth Section of Bull Market - July 26, 1934 to November 20, 1935:

The 30 Industrial Averages advanced from 84½ on July 26, 1934 to 149½ on November 20, 1935, an advance of nearly 65 points in nearly 16 months. Time, 42 months since July 1932 low; 33 months from February 1933 low 25 months from October 1933 low.

The greatest reactions were from August 25, 1934 to September 17, 1934, a decline of 12 points and from February 18, 1935 to March 18, 1935, a decline of 12 points on the averages, and as this reaction lasted only one month, it showed main trend was still up. After March 18, 1935 lows, there was no reaction over 8 points and none lasted more than 2 weeks until top was reached on November 20, 1935. Then a reaction followed to December 19, lasting one month, a decline of 11 points. The volume of sales in October and November were 104,000,000 shares, which indicated at least temporary top, with the Averages up 109 points from 1932 low, and up 53½ points from March 18, 1935 low in a period of 247 days.

At the writing, December 31, 1935, it is my opinion that the Averages will not cross 150 and when they decline to 138, will indicate 120, possibly 112, the old top of 1933-1934, but as I have said before, follow the trend of individual stocks as you trade as many of them will go opposite the trend of the 30 Industrial Averages.

TIME PERIODS TO WATCH FOR FUTURE CHANGES IN TREND

January 1936 will be 42 months from 1932 low; March 1936, 37 months from February 1933 low; July 1935 will be 36 months from the 1933 top and 48 months from the 1932 low. Therefore, these months will be very important in 1936 to watch for changes in trend.

CAUSE OF THE 1929-1932 PANIC

The price decline from 1929 to 1932 was so drastic because people who bought at high levels held on and hoped and bought more to average on the way down. They were wrong at the time they bought the first stock and continued to be wrong by bucking the trend and buying more to average, the worst thing that any trader can do. Remember, average your profits, but never average a loss.

After stocks had declined 100 points or more, other people began to buy stocks because they thought they were cheap - and the only reason they thought they were cheap was because they were down 100 points compared with high levels. This was the worst reason of all for buying stocks. Later, when stocks were down around 150, 250 and 300 points from 1929 top levels, other people bought for the same reason, that they were a long distance down from the top and looked. They were wrong because there had been no change in trend. The time period had not run out and the market had not given buying signals.

If these buyers had only waited, and had known how to follow the rules laid down in my books, WALL STREET STOCK SELECTOR and TRUTH OF THE STOCK TAPE, they could have determined when the trend changed and could have bought stocks at low levels and made big profits, but most of them were buying on guesswork and hoping that the stocks would go up. Many of these people, no doubt, made up their mind to sell out when a rally came, but fixed a price at which stocks never rallied to. They hoped for a rally, but the hope was not based on any sound reasons and there was no sound reason for expecting a rally or any advance that would let them out.

Hope Gives Way to Despair: Finally, in the spring and summer of 1932, when stocks had declined to what looked like ridiculously low levels, they continued to decline from 25 to 50 points more. This caused all kinds of buyers and investors to lose hope. Their hearts grew sick. Fear supplemented hope. They saw things in the very worst way and all sold out. Some sold because they were forced to sell, because they could not put up margins to carry their stocks. Others sold because they feared stocks would go lower, which was no reason for selling, no more than when they bought because they hoped they would go up, which was no reason for buying.

"WHO BOUGHT STOCKS IN THE PANIC?"

Many people ask this question. The people who bought stocks at low levels were those wise ones who sold out in 1928 or early 1929, or sold after the first break in September 1929, when the signs were plain that the trend had turned down. These people kept their money and waited until conditions looked the worst; they bought stocks when they were far below their actual value. They received a rich reward for their patience, knowledge and nerve, for it took nerve to buy when everything looked the worse, just as it took nerve to sell in 1929 when everything looked the brightest and one could hear nothing but optimistic talk.

"WILL STOCKS GO BACK TO 1929 HIGHS?"

This is another question that I have been asked from time to time. Why do people ask this question? Because many of them hold stocks bought at very high levels and hope that they will go up so they can get out without a loss. I am confident that the Dow-Jones Industrial 30 Averages will never sell at 386 again. I am also confident that the Railroad Averages will never sell at 189, the high of 1929, and that many of the public utility stocks will never reach the 1929 levels again. Why? Because at the time they sold out at these abnormally high levels, their selling price was not based on value or earning power. Prices were forced to these high levels for the simple reason that everybody was gambling mad and buying regardless of price or value. They will not buy stocks like that again for a long time to come because high margin requirements will restrict larger buying operation.

While I do not expect the Averages and old-time leaders to reach the 1929 highs again, yet many individual stocks will advance above their 1929 highs. During the 1932-1935 Bull Market new leaders developed that went far above the 1929 highs. In another chapter we give you examples of stocks that crossed 1929 highs and show you their position and how plain the indications were that they were going higher and the ones to buy. Other stocks, later on, will beyond their 1929 highs, as will be explained in the following chapters.

CHAPTER IV

INDIVIDUAL STOCKS vs. AVERAGES

For years, the Dow-Jones Industrial Averages, the Railroad Averages, and the Public Utility Averages have been a reliable guide to the trend of the market. Years ago when there were 12 Industrial Stocks which were representative, they were a guide to the trend of industrial stocks. When Railroads were the leaders and active, the 20 Railroad Averages were a good trend indicator. But now, since more than 1200 stocks are listed on the New York Stock Exchange, the 20 Railroad Averages and the 30 Industrial Averages are no longer representative or a guide to the average trend of the entire market.

Various industries throughout the country are affected by changing conditions and are also affected by varying conditions in foreign countries. One motor company may be prospering and making money while another one is going into bankruptcy and out of business. Crosscurrents in the stock market, due to various influences, cause some stocks to decline while others advance. These changed conditions began in 1928 and 1929, but have been more pronounced since stocks made low in July 1932. Therefore, in order to make money trading in the stock market, you must study and apply rules to individual stocks and not depend on Averages.

We do not have a universal bull market any more, when all stocks advance at the same time. We have a mixed trend, the main trend being up on some stocks and completely downward on others. The majority of stocks reached low levels in July 1932, and started working higher. The Dow-Jones 30 Industrials made low in 1932. The 20 Railroad Averages made low in June and July 1932. In 1935, at the time the Dow-Jones 30 Industrial Averages were up 80 points, the Public Utility Averages reached a new low level. This was brought about by adverse legislation.

By studying and applying the rules to individual stocks, you would have found that the Public Utility stocks showed downtrend while other stocks advanced. A study on the chart of American Telephone & Telegraph, which help up better than the other Public Utilities in 1935, revealed that it was in a stronger position. One reason was that during the entire Depression, American Telephone & Telegraph never passed its dividends and continued to pay $9 a share per year, while the other Public Utility stocks passed their dividends. During the boom, which culminated in 1929, the Public Utility stocks had been watered; stock dividends had been declared; there had been numerous split-ups. The result was that no other stock had been more overbought than the Public Utilities.

You cannot detect the best stock to buy the following the averages of any group of stocks. Some of the stocks in a group will make new highs every year in bull markets, while others will make new lows in bull markets, or go into receivership or be taken off the Exchange. For example, in 1932, when the average of all airplane stocks showed uptrend, if you had selected Curtis Wright "A" as the best airplane stock in this group to buy just because it had been a leader in a previous campaign, you would have made a mistake. In August 1932, Curtis Wright "A" sold as low as 1½; in April 1934 made a high of 12. Now compare Douglas Aircraft and make a study of its position. In 1932, Douglas made a low of 51 in February; 1934 reached a high of 28½; in September 1934 declined to 14½, a decline of about 50% from the top. In July 1935, when Curtis Wright "A" was selling 4 points under the 1934 high, Douglas crossed its 1934 top, which showed that it was in a strong position and much better to buy, even at 28½, than Curtis Wright "A". In December 1935, Douglas crossed 45½, the 1929 high, and advance to 58 while Curtis Wright "A" only advanced to 12¼. Curtis Wright "A" never showed the activity or the power to advance as Douglas and some other airplane stocks. Douglas was making higher bottoms and higher tops right along while Curtis Wright "A" was moving in a narrow trading range, so Douglas was the stock in this group to buy. This is proof that you must study each individual stock in a group in order to detect its trend.

THE DOW THEORY OBSOLETE

To make a success, you must be up to date; must discard old theories and old ideas when they become obsolete, follow new rules and new stocks in order to make a success trading in the stock market.

During recent years, the Dow Theory has spread all over the country. People have begun to regard it as very valuable and infallible, but in fact, it is now practically of no value to a trader. With so many stocks listed on the New York Stock Exchange, 30 stocks or 20 stocks are no longer representative of the trend. Besides, you cannot trade in averages. You must follow the trend of individual stocks in order to make money.

The Dow Theory worked quite will up until 1916 when the World War changed everything. Then this country changed from an agricultural country to a manufacturing country. In 1916, when the Dow-Jones 30 Industrial Averages advanced to new high levels, which was 7 points above the highs of 1906, the Railroad Averages at that time were 24 points under the 1906 record high. The man who waited for the Rails to confirm the upward trend in Industrials certainly got left and missed opportunities and probably lost money.

In 1917 the Government took over the Railroads, and in December 1917 the Dow-Jones 20 Railroad Averages declined to 69. The Industrials at the same time made a low of 66: this was the first time that that Rails were as low as they were in 1897, while the Industrials were 13 points above the 1907 panic lows.

In 1918 and 1919 the Rails failed to follow the Industrials and were no good as a guide or conformation according to the Dow Theory. In July 1919, the Industrials made a new high record while the Rails were making new low levels. In November 1919, the Industrials reached a new high at 119½. In the same month the Railroad Averages reached low of the year, only 3 points above the 1907 lows. The Rails were going exactly opposite to the trend of Industrials and the Dow Theory was not working.

In June 1921, the Railroad Averages reached a low of 64. In August 1921 the Industrials reached the same low of 64. The Industrial

Averages were only 2 points under the 1907 lows. Then followed a big bull market in Industrial stocks and the Rails were laggards.

In January 1925 the Industrial Averages crossed 120, the record high f 1919 and the Rails were still 38 points below the 1906 highs and 12 points below the 1916 highs. If you had to wait for the Rails to confirm the Industrials by making new highs before buying Industrial stocks, you would have missed big opportunities and would have had to wait until July 1927 when the Rails crossed the highs made in 1906. The Industrial Averages at that time were 63 points above the 1909 highs and 80 points above the 1906 highs for Industrial stocks.

On September 3, 1929 the 30 Industrial Averages reached the highest price in history at 386and the Rails reached a high of 189. After the panicky decline to November 1929, the Industrial Averages rallied to nearly 100 points. The Rails rallied only 29 points. After April 1930, the rails were weaker than Industrials and had smaller rallies.

In November 1931, the Rails broke 42, the low made in August 1896. In June 1932, the Rails declined to 13⅛ while the 30 Industrial Averages declined to 40½. The Industrials were 12 points above the 1896 lows, while the Rails were 29 points under the 1896 lows.

In July 1933, the Industrials rallied to 110 and the Rails rallied to 58.

In October 1933, the Industrial Averages reacted to 82½ and the Rails to 33. The Industrials never broke the 1933 lows until they advanced to 149½ in November 1935.

In March 1935, the Rails sold at 27 while the Industrials were at 96. The Industrials were 13 points above the lows of October 1933, while the Rails were 6 points below. This again proved that you could not depend upon the Dow Theory.

From March 1935 to November 1935, the Industrials advanced to 53½ points while the Rails rallied only 12 points. You would have missed profits of anywhere from 50 to 75 points if you had waited to buy Industrial stocks until the Rails made new highs and confirmed the advance.

This is plenty of proof that the Dow Theory is now obsolete and that you cannot depend upon it to work in the future.

CHANGE WITH THE TIMES

In order to make money under the changed conditions, you must study individual stocks and follow their trend. Don't let the Averages fool you. When one stock shows a change in trend, go with it regardless of the others in the same group and regardless of the action of the Averages.

Years ago the Stage Coach Stocks advanced and you could have made money buying them, but stage coaches went out of business and so did the stocks. Then there were Canal Stocks that advanced and you could have made money buying them, but other modes of transportation reduced the business on canals. The automobiles came along and took business away from the railroads. Now the airplane is coming along and taking business from the railroads and will later take it from the automobiles and trucks. The airplane will be the future mode of transportation. You will have to watch airplanes in future for a guide, the same as you watched automobile stocks a few years ago, because the money will be made trading in airplane stocks rather than rails or automobiles.

Keep up to date: be progressive. Do no cling to old theories or ideas. Learn to follow the trend of individual stocks and you will make profits.

WHERE TO BUY AND SELL

You should buy a stock near a single bottom, a double bottom, or a triple bottom and place a stop loss order not more than 3 points away. By buying near a single bottom, I mean that after a reaction you should wait until a stock holds around a level for 2 to 3 weeks, then buy and protect with a stop loss order 3 points under the lowest week, or in active markets if a stock reacts and then holds around a level for 2 to 3 days, buy and protect with a stop loss order not more than 3 points under the lowest day. When a stock sells around the same price level several weeks, several months, or a year or more apart, it forms a double bottom and is a buy. If it sells around the same level the third time, it is a triple bottom.

When a stock advances to a new high level or crosses a former old top by 3 points, then if it is going higher, it should not react back 3 points below the former old high. Then you should buy on a slight reaction of 1 to 3 points and place a stop loss order 3 points under the old top.

After a bull market gets started, buy on a reaction and place a stop loss order 3 points under the previous support level.

After a stock crosses the top of a previous year by 3 points, it is a buy on any little reaction. For example:

Douglas Aircraft: 1932 high 18⅝. 1933 high 18¼. In 1934, when it crossed this double top, according to the rule, you would buy. The stock advanced to 28½ in 1934. Then in 1935, after Douglas Aircraft crossed 28½, it never reacted lower than 26½. Therefore, when it reacted back below 28, it was a buy with a stop at 25½. It is significant to note that after Douglas crossed the old high of 28½, it never reacted 3 days (the reactions only lasting about 2 days) before the stock resumed its upward trend. When it crossed the 1929 high at 45½, you would buy again and continue to pyramid as long as it showed uptrend. The stock advanced to 58⅜ in December 1935.

Reverse the above rules on the selling side. You should sell against single tops, double tops, or triple tops, or at some point where you can place a stop loss order not more than 3 points away, or wait until a stock shows distribution and breaks the last important bottom by 3 points, then sell short on a small rally and place a stop loss order 3 points above the old bottom. After a stock breaks the bottom of a previous year by 3 points, it is a short sale.

In a bear market, when a stock declines and breaks an old bottom by 3 points or more, then if it is going lower it should not rally 3 points above the old bottom before it goes lower. For example:

United Fruit: This stock made a low of 84⅞ in May 1935 and a low of 84¼ in June 1935; rallied to 90¾ in July, and after it broke 81 or 3 points under these previous lows, it never rallied 3 points above them until it declined to 60½ in October 1935.

Whatever you do, it should be according to a definite rule and after the market shows a definite trend. Wait for as sure an indication to buy or sell as you can possibly get. Don't get impatient and jump into the market just because you want to make a trade. Remember, a stock is never too high to buy so long the trend is up, provided you place a stop loss order for protection in case the trend reverses. A stock is a short sale at any time and at any price so long as the trend is down, regardless of how high it has been previously.

PRICE AT WHICH FAST MOVES START

The higher the price, the faster a stock moves and the wider the fluctuations. Stocks move up faster after they sell above 50 and even faster after they sell above 100, and when they get above 150 and 200 per share, the fluctuations are very wide and rapid. You can prove this to yourself by going over any of the stocks that have been active and had big advances and see what happened after they crossed 50, after they crossed 100, and after went above 150 and 200.

The same on a decline: Stocks move down rapidly from the extreme high prices in the first 50 to 100 points' decline from the top. After a stock gets below 100 the moves are somewhat smaller, and when it gets below 50, they are even smaller and rallies are also smaller, especially if the stock has had a big decline. The lower they get, the less they rally.

TIME TO HOLD AFTER BUYING OR SELLING

After you make a trade, if the stock closes showing you a loss the first day, you are apt to be wrong and trading against the trend. If it closes against you the third successive day, you are wrong nine times out of ten and should get out of this trade immediately.

When you buy or sell and the trade immediately moves in your favor and closes with a profit the first day, you are right and with the trend. At the end of three days, if it still shows you a profit, it is almost a sure sign that you are right and with the main trend.

Therefore, get out at once when you see that you are wrong and hold when you see that you are right.

BUYING OUTRIGHT FROM 1929 TO 1932

I have written in all of my former books that it never pays to buy stocks outright because it does not help any if the trend happens to go against you. I have stated that the only time it is safe to buy stocks outright is when they are selling around $10 per share or lower. So many people get the mistaken idea that because they have a stock paid for they cannot lose on it. That is just where they are wrong. When you buy a stock outright, you do not worry because you think you will not have a margin call, but you also fail to realize the fact that you can lose all the money that you pay for the stock, because it can go to nothing and be assessed. Therefore, when you make a trade, the idea is to know what you are going to do if it goes against you. You should protect it with a stop loss order and limit your risk. Holding on and hoping never helped anyone and never will. When you are wrong, get out at the market and take a small loss, but when the market moves in your favor, hold on for big profits. Don't think that because you are well acquainted with a stock and because it has gone up for many bull campaigns in the past, that it will go up in the future, because old leaders go and new ones come to take their places. You must keep up to date in the market and buy and sell the new leaders in order to make profits.

WATCH BOTTOMS AND TOPS OF PREVIOUS CAMPAIGNS

When a stock breaks the bottom of the previous bear campaign by 3 points, then you should watch for support around the bottom of the next former campaign. For example:

When stocks started down in 1929, you should watch the bottoms of 1923-24, the previous campaign. Then if those lows were broken, you should watch the bottoms of the 1921 campaign, from which the great Bull Market started. If these bottoms were broken by 3 points, the next lows would be 1917, then 1914, and after that the 1907 panic lows, then 1903-04 and 1896 extreme lows.

You should look up each individual stock and see what years it made its previous extreme lows. When you find that a stock has reached the extreme low of its history and then holds for several weeks or several months and fails to break the old bottom by 3 points, you judge that it is in a strong position and time to buy with a stop loss order 3 points under the old low level.

Industrial Averages: In 1932, after the Averages broke the low of 85, which was made in 1931, the next important bottom to watch was the low of 64 in 1921. The Averages declined to 70 in 1932, and held for some time, but finally declined and broke the low of 64. Then you would look for the next bottom and would find that in 1907 and 1914 these Averages made a low at 53. When they declined and broke 53 in 1932, the support level of these two panicky declines, you would have to look for the next bottom, which was 43 in 1903, from which a big bull campaign started. In July 1932 the Dow-Jones Industrial Averages declined to 40½, failing to get 3 points under the 1903 low, a sign of support. The market became dull and narrow, the volume of sales dropped to the lowest of any time since 1929, accumulation took place and the trend turned up again from that point.

In an extreme bear campaign, like 1929-32, when a stock declines back to the old levels made 20 to 30 years before, then holds without breaking these previous panic levels by 3 points, it indicates that it is receiving support and that it is a buy with a stop loss order 3 points under the old low level.

U.S. Steel is an example. In June 1932, it declined to 21¼, which was only ⅝ point lower than the extreme low in the 1907 panic. It was a buy protected with a stop loss order at 19. A rally followed from that level, but U.S. Steel did not have so big an advance from 1932 to 1935 as other stocks because it had been split up and the amount of stock increased from 5 million shares to over 8 million shares.

It is just as important to watch old tops of previous campaigns. The further back they are, the more important when they are crossed by 3 points. For example:

Westinghouse Electric made a low of 38½ in 1918 and a low of 40½ in 1919. In 1921 the low was 38⅞, selling around the same level for 3 years.
This showed strong support and indicated that the stock was being accumulated for much higher prices. It continued to work higher and in 1925 crossed the 1915 high at 74⅞ and advanced to 84, which showed that it was going higher. The next top to watch was the high of 116½ in 1902, the highest of its history up to that time. When it crossed this level it indicated much higher prices, and according to the rule, you would continue to pyramid all the way up. The stock sold at 292⅝ in 1929.

Follow the trend of each individual stock in the same way and when it crosses the top of a previous year or the tops of previous campaigns by 3 points, it is an indication that the stock is going higher.

In a bear campaign you should watch tops of former campaigns as well as bottoms of previous campaigns. In the bull market that culminated in November 1916, the Dow-Jones Industrial Averages reached a new high level of 100, then followed a sharp decline. In 1919 these averages made anther new high just under 120; then in the panicky decline in 1921 reached 64. After the bull market culminated in 1929, there was a sharp decline in October 1931 and the averages broke 3 points under 120, the old 1919 top, which was an indication of lower prices. Then we would watch the next top at 110. When the averages broke 3 points under that top, they declined to 85 in October 1931. Then on November 9, 1931, rallied back to 119 or around the old top at 120. When they

41

failed to cross this old top, it was an indication that the stocks were still in a bear market and that prices were going lower.

HOW TO DETECT EARLY LEADERS IN A BEAR MARKET

Stocks which advance fast and make top and are distributed before other stocks reach top indicate that they will be early leaders in a bear market.

When stocks break the bottoms of previous years or the low point for several months previous, ahead of other stocks, they indicate that they will be early leaders on the decline.

In every bear market there are early leaders or stocks that decline first and reach bottom ahead of the general list of stocks. For example:

Chrysler Motors: In March 1926, Chrysler Motors sold at 28½. The big bull market followed and in October 1928 it reached extreme high at 140½. This was 11 months before the Dow-Jones Averages and the general market made top in September 1929. You could have been short of Chrysler while other stocks were advancing. Many motor stocks did not reach high until August and September 1929.

It is important to study and see what happened to Chrysler in 1929 while the big advance in other stocks was taking place. Look at the Monthly and Weekly Charts. In January 1929 Chrysler high 135; trend turned down and in May 1929, it declined to 66, down 74½ points from the 1928 high. August 1929, high of the rally 79, still down 61 points from October 1928 high. Then, when the great crash followed in October and November, Chrysler, which already showed downtrend and was in a weak position, declined to 26 in November 1929. On April 1930, high of the rally 43, which showed weakness because it failed to have any big rally. June 1932, low 5. Stayed around the low level for 3 months, down 135 points from the high of October 1928.

When a stock advances sharply in the first or second year of a bull market and makes top and then fails for two years to cross the top made in the first or second year of a bull market, it is a sure sign of weakness and the stock should be sold short when it shows that the trend had

42

turned down again. You can detect this change in trend by watching the Monthly and Weekly Charts. For example:

Corn Products was one of the stocks that was an early leader in 1933. In August and September 1933, Corn Products advanced and made top at 90⅝. In August 1934, it declined to 56; then showed accumulation and the trend turned up again, but when the advance started in March 1935, Corn Products moved up slower than it had in 1933. In July 1935, it reached a high of 78⅜. By studying the Weekly Chart and the Daily Chart, it was easy to see that Corn Products had made top. It failed by 12 points to the reach the high of August and September 1933, which showed that the selling was better than the buying. In October 1935, it declined to a low of 60, down 18 points from the high of July 1935 high, and in July 1933 reached a high of 90, the same as in 1929, and failed to cross this level. This being a double top is where you should have sold out longs and gone short with a stop 3 points above the 1929 high. July 1934, low 20¾; December high 34¾; June 1935 low 22½. Holding 1¾ points above the previous bottom, it showed good support. It held for 7 months between 23 and 28, and in October 1935 crossed 28, showing uptrend; in November 1935 crossed the December 1934 high at 34¾. It will have to advance 3 points above that level to indicate higher prices.

U.S. Smelting: This was another early leader that showed plainly ahead of time that it was going to have a big advance. April 1929 high, 72⅞; September 1931 low 12⅜; in November rallied to 26; June 1933 extreme low 10, which was the lowest in its history. Note the Yearly Chart: 1907 low 24¼; 1915 low 20; 1916 high 81½, the record price up to that time; 1923 low 18; 1929 high 72⅞, making lower tops since 1916; then in June 1932 made an all-time low.

Big accumulation took place in a narrow trading range. In April 1933, U.S. Smelting crossed 26, above all tops back to 1930. Here you should start buying and would pyramid as the stock worked higher. A fast advance followed. In July 1933 it crossed 73, the 1292 high, a sure indication for much higher prices and a place to buy more; then crossed 81, the high of 1916, the highest in its history. Here would have been the place to buy more stock and continue to pyramid. In 1933, September, October and November made highs around 105, and in February 1934 crossed 105, where you would buy again. It reached the extreme high of 141 in July 1934, up 131 points from its low, at the time when other stocks were making bottoms. After this quick advance against the trend of the general market, the stock worked lower, showing downtrend, while other stocks still showed uptrend. In September and December 1935, it sold at 92.

U.S. Industrial Alcohol: In June 1932, it made a low of 13¼; advanced in September 1932 to 36; then on the secondary decline in February 1933, declined to a low of 13½, holding one-half point above the 1932 low. This double bottom was a sign of strength and a place to buy. In 1933, in July, U.S. Industrial Alcohol advanced to 94. This was due to the Repeal of the 18th Amendment and an over-estimate by the public of the earnings that whiskey stocks and other industrial alcohol companies could make. The public went wild and bought too high. This sharp advance from a low of 13½ in February 1933 to a high of 94 in July 1933, was entirely too fast and the movement collapsed. In September 1934, U.S. Industrial Alcohol rallied to 47. After that is was a slow mover, lagged behind the market and did not cross 47 again until September 1935.

If you had followed the trend, you would have bought this stock all the way up in 1933 and then as soon as the trend turned down on the Weekly Chart, you would begin to sell it short.

United Fruit: In July 1932, extreme low 10¼. Showed good accumulation, turned trend up and indicated that it would be an early leader when it crossed the 1932 high at 32⅜ in March 1933. It was a good leader in 1933, 1934, and in early 1935. 1933 high 68; 1934 high 77; May 1935 high 92¾. As long as it continued to make higher bottoms and higher tops, you would buy, but when the trend turned down in July 1935, ahead of other stocks, you would follow the trend and sell it short.

Chrysler Motors: In July 1932, extreme low 5; September 1932, high 21¾. March 1933 declined to 7¾, a higher bottom than 1932 by 2¾ points, a sign of strength and accumulation and a good place to buy. April 1933, Chrysler started activity on increased volume and in May crossed the 1932 top, a sure sign of higher prices. Then crossed the 1931 high at 25¾ and the 1930 high at 43. February 1934, high 60⅜ on big volume of sales. The Daily and Weekly Charts showed that this was

44

top and the trend turned down. August and September 1934, Chrysler sold at 29¼. As it held nearly half of the advance from the 1932 low to the 1934 high, it was in strong position. March 1935, made another bottom at 31, holding 1¾ points above the 1934 level, a double bottom, a sign of good support and time to buy. August 1935 it crossed the old 1934 top at 60⅜, a sure indication of higher prices and a place to buy more. December 1935, advanced to 93⅞. From the low in March 1935 to the high in December 1935, Chrysler advanced 62⅞ points and at no time reacted more than 9 points, a wonderful opportunity to pyramid, which was plainly shown all the time by the strong uptrend.

HOW TO DETECT STOCKS IN STRONG POSITION

It is easy to pick the stocks in strong position if you follow the rules laid down in TRUTH OF THE STOCK TAPE and WALL STREET STOCK SELECTOR and the rules in NEW STOCK TREND DETECTOR. Example:

Westinghouse: June 1932, low 15⅝, the same low as 1907. According to our rule, this was a place to buy with a stop 3 points under the old bottom. September 1932, high 43½; February 1933, low 19⅜, a higher bottom by 3¾ points, showing good support. The stock remained in a dull, narrow trading range for some time, and by the rules for detecting a change in trend you would discern that this was accumulation and would buy the stock. One reason why you should be watching Westinghouse was that this stock was never split up and never declared a stock dividend during the 1929 boom.

In July 1933, Westinghouse crossed 43½, the top of September 1932. This was an indication for higher prices and you should have bought more when it crossed the old top. It advanced to 58¾ in July 1933. The Daily and Weekly Charts showed at that time, that it was making top and you would sell out and go short. In October 1933, it declined to 28⅝, making a higher bottom by 9¼ points than February 1933, still showing a strong uptrend. Then it held for a long time in a narrow trading range with a small volume of sales, a sign of accumulation, and failed to break the bottom at 28⅝.

It advanced in February 1934 to a high of 47¼, where again there was large volume and the Daily and Weekly Charts showed that it was making top and that it was time to get out and go short, as the trend of most stocks turned down after February 1934, when the trading was running at the rate of 5,000,000 shares per day after stocks had had a big advance. In July 1934, Westinghouse declined to 27⅞, only ¾ point lower than the bottom of October 1933, and if you bought around 29, the old bottom, with a 3-point stop loss order at 26, the stop would not have been caught. After the low of July 1934, Westinghouse remained in a narrow trading range until December 1934, a sign of accumulation. A detective who had been watching this stock would have seen clear signs of accumulation when it failed to break the old bottom by one point, and would have bought the stock.

In March 1935, when most all of the stocks reacted and the Dow-Jones Industrial Averages made bottom, Westinghouse declined to a low of 32⅝; then activity started and volume of sales increased. In April 1935, it crossed 47¼, the 1934 top, a strong indication of higher prices and a place to buy more.

In July 1935, Westinghouse crossed 58¾, the 1933 high, another strong indication of higher prices and a place to buy. According to our rule, it should not decline 3 points under this old top, which would be 55, in order to maintain a strong uptrend. After it crossed 58¾, it reacted to 57 only and then advanced to 98¾ in November 1935. This was a good stock to pyramid as it showed uptrend all the way from March 1935 to November 1935.

NEW LOWS LATE IN A BEAR CAMPAIGN

When stocks decline late in a bear campaign, or after a prolonged decline which has run two or three years, and break into new low levels, they are not likely to decline as far as they would if they broke into new low levels early in the campaign. Your rule should be that after a stock declines to new low levels and then rallies back 3 points above the old bottom, it is an indication that the decline is over, that liquidation has been completed, and that the stock is getting ready to turn up again.

American Tel. & Tel.: 1907 panic, low 88. In June 1932, it broke 88 after the bear market had run 33 months and in July 1932 declined to 70¼, or 17¾ points lower than the old low of 1907, but later in the same month rallied and closed at 89½, above the old low of 88. The decline below 88 was a final wave of liquidation and the quick rally that followed was an indication that final bottom had been reached. In August, the stock advanced to 91, or 3 points above the old low of 88, an indication of higher prices; then in September 1932, advanced to 121. Following the rule, you would have bought American Tel. & Tel. at 91, when it was 3 points above the old bottom at 88, even though it was up 20 points from the extreme low, and then would have made 30 points on it in less than 2 months. Another proof that you should always follow the rules and go with the trend of an individual stock and change when the trend changes.

Consolidated Gas: This is another stock that had a final wave of liquidation in 1934-1935 when other stocks had crossed previous highs. 1932 low, 56⅛. In 1932, it broke 56⅛ and declined to 32; rallied to 66 in September 1932. Then in July 1934 it broke 32, the low of 1932, and declined to 15⅞ in February 1935; rallied to 34½ in August 1935 and 34¾ in November. When it failed to get 3 points above the 1932 low of 32, a sign of weakness, you should have sold out and gone short. It declined to 25⅝ in September 1935. When it can cross 35, or get 3 points above the old low, it will then indicate higher prices.

NEW HIGHS LATE IN 1929 BULL MARKET

The Dow-Jones 30 Industrial Averages made the extreme high on September 3, 1929 and U.S. Steel and many other leading stocks reached high on that date, but very few people know who do not take the trouble to keep up records that after the big crash in September 1929, some stocks were still working higher and made high of the year in early October 1929.

Timken Roller Bearing: The high for Timken during September 1929 was 119½. Extreme high of 139⅜ reached in October 1929: It made 20 points higher in October, while Averages had declined 100 points from the high in September.

U.S. Industrial Alcohol: September 1929 high, 226½. Early October 1929, high 243⅝, making a top 17 points higher in October than September, despite the heavy selling and the smash in the general market. The time was not yet up for this late mover to make top, and, therefore, it advanced against the trend of the Averages.

You would have made a mistake if you had sold Timken Roller Bearing and U.S. Industrial Alcohol short just because the Averages and other stocks had turned down and were short sales, but if you followed the rule and bought these stocks according to the trend, as indicated, you would have been long of them until they reached top and gave a signal for downtrend.

NEW HIGHS FOLLOWING YEAR AFTER END OF BULL CAMPAIGN

After market reaches final top of a bull campaign, usually there is a sharp, quick decline, then a secondary rally, from which a prolonged bear market follows. After the extreme top in September 1929, there was a panicky decline in October and November, one of the worst in history. Then stocks advanced and made a secondary top in April 1930, with the Dow-Jones Industrial Averages nearly 100 points lower than the 1929 tops. Yet, a few stocks made these extreme highs in April 1930.

It is interesting to study what kind of stocks recorded new highs and determine why they made them. Most of the stocks, which advanced into a new high territory in April 1930, were stocks that had a small amount of stock outstanding and were easy to manipulate. When these stocks crossed the 1929 highs, they certainly indicated higher and you should have followed their trend up until they indicated top, even though other stocks were still in a bear market and selling far below the 1929 highs.

Coca Cola: This stock, which had been split up in 1929, advanced in 1930 and did not reach high until June 1930. It recorded a high of 191⅜ at that time. In view of the fact that it had been late in making its top, it would naturally be late in making a bottom. While many stocks, in fact the majority of stocks, made low in July 1932, Coca Cola declined and

48

did not make low until December 1932, when it sold at 68½; then showed accumulation and the main trend turned up. It continued to work higher each year, making higher bottoms and higher tops, until it advanced to 298½ in November 1935and was again split up 4 for 1.

Electric Power & Light: In the panicky decline of November 1929, this stock sold at a low of 29⅛; in April 1930 made a high of 103½, up 17 points above the high of September 1929. After it crossed September 1929 high, you should have followed the trend up until it showed signs of turning down. Then, when it broke back under the September 1929 top and showed downtrend, you should have followed it down on the short side just the same as any other stock.

In July 1932, Electric Power & Light declined to 2¾. In September 1933 it advanced to 16; the worked lower in 1933, 1934, and 1935. When other stocks advanced in 1934 and 1935 and this stock failed to cross the high of September 1933, it indicated a short sale. In March 1935, when the Public Utility Stocks were under pressure due to adverse legislation, Electric Power & Light reached an extreme low of 1⅛. Therefore, as this stock was working down and making new lows from time to time, showing downtrend, you should have been following its trend and selling short.

Vanadium Steel: February 1929 high, 116½. April 1930 high, 143¼. April 1935, low 11¼. One of the reasons why this stock advanced to such a high level in April 1930 was because there was a small available supply of stock and a small number of shared outstanding. At that time, the directors of the company made a lot of money speculating in stocks. Then followed poor business and the company during the Depression got into a bad financial condition. After the stock declined to 11¼ in April 1935, it worked up very slowly, being a late move in working up just as it was in 1930, because the steel business was slow and the last to recover from the Depression.

National Steel: It is important to compare the position of this stock, which has a small floating supply, with other steel stocks. This company showed good earnings during the Depression, much better than Vanadium or even U.S. Steel. National Steel was a late mover and made top in April 1930 at 76½. July 1932, low 13½. It made higher bottoms in 1933, 1934, and 1935. In July 1935, it crossed the high of

49

February 1934, an indication of higher prices and a point to buy more. In November 1935, advanced above the top of April 1930. This company with its small capitalization is well managed and has a far better future than U.S. Steel, Bethlehem Steel and some others, but you must always follow the trend of a stock, regardless of what you think about it, and when the trend turns down, you should follow it down.

STOCKS THAT CROSSED 1929 HIGHS

I have stated before that I did not expect the Averages to ever sell at the 1929 high again, but that individual stocks from time to time would cross their 1929 highs and make new highs. For example:

American Safety Razor: June 1932, low 13⅜. It worked higher in 1933 and 1934 and never had more than two or three months' reaction. In 1935, February, March and April, held around 75, the 1929 top. May 1935, crossed 75, which was a sure sign of higher prices as it was in the new high territory. July 1935, advanced to 95¾. This stock showed uptrend all the way from 1932 and was an early leader. You should have bought it right along and then bought more when it crossed the 1929 high.

By comparing Gillette with American Safety Razor, you will see what would have happened if you had bought this stock to follow American Safety Razor. In September 1933, Gillette made a new low at 7⅝; then held in a very narrow trading range. It reached low of 12 in August 1935.

Columbia Pictures: Aril 1930, high 54¾. December 1931, low 2⅝. This stock made low six months before other stocks. In July 1932, when other stocks reached extreme low, Columbia Pictures crossed tops and already showed uptrend. March 1933, low 6⅝, showing good support 4 points higher than the 1931 low. May 1933, crossed the 1932 high, a sure sign of higher prices. In July 1935, it sold at 81. While Paramount, Radio-Keith-Orpheum, and Warner Brothers' stocks in the moving-picture line were in the hands of receivers and holding at low levels, this stock was working up. Always buy the stocks in strong position and leave those in weak position alone.

Congoleum: December 1930, low 6¼. It showed a long level of accumulation and made last low at 7½ in March 1933; then continued to make higher bottoms and higher tops until July 1935, when it crossed the 1929 high at 35¾.

McKeesport Tin Plate: July 1932, extreme low 28; September high, 56⅝; December low, 40⅛; and in February 1933, when other stocks were at low levels, it advanced to 57, above the September 1932 top, a sure sign of much higher prices. Extreme high had been 103½ in 1931. It showed in the early stages of the campaign that it was in a straight-up bull market and a real leader. In August 1933, it made a high of 95¾; in October reacted to 67¼; February 1934, high 94¼; July 1934, low 79, raising bottoms all the time. In April 1935, when it crossed the 1931 high, it was easy to detect that it was in a strong position and making for a new high.

National Distillers: June 1929, high 58½; October 1929, low 15; June 1932, low 13, making a double bottom against May 1926 low at 12½ and holding only 2 points under the low of October 1929, an indication of strong support. Big accumulation took place, and while other stocks were making new lows right along, this stock was holding up. August 1932, high 27¼; February 1933, low 16⅞. This higher bottom indicated that it was getting ready to advance to higher levels. In April 1933, it crossed the 1932 high at 27¼ and 1931 high at 36⅜, another sure sign for higher prices, where you should buy it and then pyramid all the way up. In May 1933, it crossed the 1928 and 1929 highs around 58, and in July 1933, reached a high of 124, when everybody got bullish and was talking 500 to 1000 for this stock; then was the time to sell out and go short. A sharp decline followed.

This shows the wisdom of following the trend of an individual stock and not the trend of the Averages or just any stock in a group.

STOCKS THAT DID NOT ADVANCE MUCH FROM 1932 TO 1935

By going over a large list of stocks, you will find many that did not advance much from 1932 to 1935; in fact, during that same period some of them made lower prices than in May to June 1932. For example:

American International: July 1932, low 2½. July 1933, high 15⅛. 1933 low 4¼, 1934 low, 4¾, 1935 low 4½. In December 1935, it was selling at 10, while other stocks that made lows around 3 to 5 in 1932 had advanced 25, 50 and 75 points. By looking at the Monthly Chart on American International you will see that it never showed that it was going to follow the advance in other stocks. Therefore, you would leave it alone and buy those that were making higher bottoms and higher tops.

Standard Gas & Electric: June 1932, low 7⅝. March 1933, low 5⅛. December 1934, low 3⅝. March 1935, low 1½. This stock made new low levels each year while other stocks were advancing and crossing former highs. In sold at 6⅜ in December 1935.

National Dairy: In June 1932, it sold at 14⅜, and in February 1933 sold at 10½. It was almost 4 points lower than the 1932 low while the Dow-Jones 30 Industrial Averages were selling 9 points higher than their 1932 lows. Then you certainly would not have bought National Dairy in March 1933, as an early leader or a stock that would advance fast, because it showed that it was in a weak position. However, it did advance in 1933, but not nearly so much as other stocks which had sold around the same low price as National Dairy.

In July 1933, it reached high at 25¾. Again the trend turned down and in December 1933, it declined to a low of 11¼, making a double bottom or slightly higher than the low of February 1933. This was a place to buy if you wanted to buy this class of stock, which is a slow mover. In July 1934, it made a high of 18¾; then in March 1935, declined to a low of 12⅞ and held in a slow trading range. The fact that it was 2 points higher than the low of December 1933 showed the stock was getting support and would eventually work up. It did not cross the 1934 high until November 1935. Therefore, you would not expect this

1935 - In July Chrysler crossed the 1934 tops at 60⅜ while Auburn was far below the 1934 top. While Auburn moved up in October 1935 to 45, Chrysler advanced to 88¾, selling at a higher level than Auburn sold in July 1933.

This is more proof that you must follow the trend of the individual stocks and buy those in the strongest position and sell short those in the weakest position.

Why did Chrysler move up much faster during 1935 than Auburn and the other motor stocks? Because it had made early high in the previous bull campaign, reaching high in October 1928; therefore, its time period was different than other stocks. Auburn made high late in the 1929 campaign; reacted to 60⅜, and then advanced to 295½ in April 1931, while other stocks were on a decline. This again proves that you must trade according to the trend of the individual stocks.

BUYING ONE STOCK AND SELLING ANOTHER SHORT AT THE SAME TIME

UNITED FRUIT AND CHRYSLER MOTORS COMPARISON

A comparison of these two stocks and their weekly high and low movements for the year 1935 is to prove to you how important it is to study individual stocks and trade according to the trend of the individual stock and not buy one stock just because some other stock is going up or sell one stock short because some other stock happens to be declining. Judge each stock according to its position and determine its individual trend and go with it.

1935

Week ended Jan. 5: United Fruit high 75½; Chrysler Motors high 42½. United Fruit 33 points higher than Chrysler.

March 16: Chrysler reached low of the year at 31; United Fruit selling at 75⅛, or 44⅛ points higher than Chrysler.

May 18: United Fruit reached extreme high of 92¾. At this time Chrysler was selling at 49⅜. United Fruit 43 points higher than Chrysler.

At this point, if you had followed the trend on Chrysler, which showed up, and had bought Chrysler, and then, when the trend showed down on United Fruit, had gone short, you would have made big profits on both deals.

August 10: United Fruit 72, down 20¾ points from the high of week ended May 18.

Chrysler 62¾, up 13⅜ points from the high of week ended May 18. At this time United Fruit was only 9¼ points higher than Chrysler.

August 24: On a reaction, Chrysler sold at 57½. United Fruit was selling at 65, only 7½ points above Chrysler.

September 14: Chrysler 74, United Fruit 74. United Fruit down 18¾ points from the top of May; Chrysler up 24⅝ points from high of week ended May 18. Here you would have had a profit of 24 points in

Chrysler if you had bought it at the time you sold United Fruit short and you would have had 18 points' profit in United Fruit. The trend was still down on United Fruit and the trend was still up on Chrysler. You would trade in both stocks according to their individual trend.

October 5: Chrysler low 69. United Fruit extreme low of the decline 60½, down 32¼ points from the high. At this time Chrysler was selling 8½ points higher than United Fruit.

November 23: Chrysler high 90, United Fruit 73½. Chrysler 16½ points higher than United Fruit.

December 28: Chrysler reached extreme high of the year at 93⅞. United Fruit again declined to 60⅞. At this time Chrysler was 33 points higher than United Fruit.

The Weekly Swing Chart on United Fruit and Chrysler shows you how these stocks were far apart and then how they worked and came together: then one worked lower and the other worked higher.

This is not the only comparison of this kind that can be made. There were many other stocks in 1935 that were declining while other stocks were advancing, but this is ample proof of the large profits that you could have been making by keeping short of United Fruit right along and at the same time pyramiding on the long side of Chrysler, buying all the way up.

By selling stocks short that are in weak position or show downtrend and buying the stocks that show uptrend, you can often make money on the short side and the long side at the same time.

As in a rule, in a bull market a stock that is going higher will not react more than two to three months and should resume the upward trend in the third month. If a stock is going lower, it will continue the decline in the third month.

Chrysler: After it sold at 28 in March 1926, it never had more than two months' decline at any time until it advanced to 140½ in October 1928. After it reached top at 140½ it never rallied over two months until it sold at 26 in November 1929, which shows you how important this rule is. In April 1930, the high was 43 and it never rallied over two months until the time it sold at 5 in June 1932.

Dow-Jones Railroad Averages: The Dow-Jones 20 Railroad Averages reached the highest in their history in September 1929 when they sold at 189. They declined sharply in the panic of November 1929; then rallied to 158 in April 1930; and declined to 13 in June 1932. The lowest prices at which these Averages sold in August 1896, was 42. Therefore, when they broke their lowest average in history, they indicated much lower prices and you should have sold railroad stocks short and followed them down until the Averages and the individual stocks that you were short of showed that they had reached bottom and that a change in trend was taking place.

One of the signs of weakness in a bear market is a rally of only six to seven weeks or not more than two months, not getting higher in the third month. From March 1930 to the low in 1932, at no time did the Railroad Averages advance over two months; and from February 1931 when the high was 111, until they declined to 13, they never rallied more than one month. This was a sign of great weakness, indicating heavy liquidation and a real panicky bear market.

SHOULD STOCKS WITH SMALL NUMBER OF SHARES OUTSTANDING BE SOLD SHORT?

In a bear market, or when the trend of a stock is down, it is just as safe to sell short stocks with a small number of shared outstanding as it is to sell short stocks with a large number of shared outstanding, because they all go down after distribution is completed, and stocks that have sold very high go very low, as was proved in the great panic of 1929 to 1932. Example:

Case Threshing Machine: With only 130,000 shares outstanding, Case advanced to 115 in November 1928; then declined to a low of 16¾ in May 1932. This stock had many sharp rallies. If you had followed the trend, sold it short as long as the trend was down, covered and went long when the trend showed up, you would have made a large amount of money as it worked down nearly 500 points from the top.

Auburn Motors: This is another example of a stock that sold at 514 in September 1929, and declined to 15 in March 1935.

Auburn had only 166,000 shares outstanding, yet it declined 499 points from the extreme high in 1929 to the extreme low in 1935. How many people would sell Auburn short after it was down to 100 and after it sold at 50? Yet, as long as the trend was down, it was a short sale even at 25 or 20. The same on the long side! A stock is good to buy no matter how high it goes as long as the trend is up. Auburn was just as good to buy at 400 when the trend was up as it was to sell short at 40 when the trend was down.

Radio Common: While this was not a stock with a small number of shares outstanding, it reached extreme high at 549 in March 1929; was split up five for one; declined to a low of 2½ in June 1932. How many people in 1929 dreamed that Radio would ever decline to 2½ again? Probably not one in a million. This decline of 546½ points in 32 months was the greatest decline in any stock from 1929 to 1932, which is certainly convincing proof that buying stocks outright never pays because they can go down to nothing. There is only one way to trade, that is, to place stop loss orders and limit risks to a few points on every stock you buy.

No matter how small or how large the volume, when the trend turns down, stocks go down, and when the trend shows up, stocks go up.

WAIT FOR DEFINITE BUYING SIGNAL AT BOTTOM

At the end of a panic or a long decline, there is always plenty of time to buy stocks at low levels. All you have to do is study past records and how stocks acted at the bottom of 1932 to prove to yourself that it requires a long time for accumulation to take place at the bottom before stocks start up. You can make money much quicker by waiting to buy when the trend turns up. After you have allowed several weeks or several months to elapse, if a stock holds bottom levels, it shows accumulation and you can buy with a stop loss order under the bottom.

Johns-Manville: This is a good example of how long a stock that has sold at very high levels, can hold at low levels. Johns-Manville sold at 242¾ in 1929. It declined to 10 in April 1932 and held around 10 in April, May, June and July 1932, accumulating for nearly 4 months at low levels. In the latter part of July 1932, Johns-Manville showed uptrend by crossing the tops of previous months and in September 1932 advanced to a high of 33⅜. This was an opportunity to make more than 20 points' profit in 60 days after you had waited three to four months to see if it would hold the bottom. You could have bought it at 10, or just above 10, and placed a stop loss order at 9, which would have held. Johns-Manville was one of the good stocks to pyramid in 1934 and 1935 because it continued to cross tops and make higher bottoms and higher tops, reaching a high of 99½ in November 1935.

It takes time for accumulation to be completed. Do not make the mistake that is made by so many traders who hang over the tape and try to catch the bottom eighth and the top eighth. They never do it and lose all of their money in the end. Do not guess and try to anticipate what the market is going to do. Wait until you detect a definite indication of a change in trend and get a definite buying signal. Do not pay any attention to averages or stocks in the same group. Remember, you must follow the trend of the individual stock.

CHAPTER VI

VOLUME OF SALES

The *Volume of Sales* is the real driving power behind the market and shows whether Supply and Demand is increasing or decreasing. Large buying or selling orders from professional traders, the public or any other source of supply and demand are bound to be registered on the tape and shown in the volume of sales.

Therefore, a careful study of the *Volume of Sales* will enable you to determine very clearly a change in trend, especially if you apply all the other rules for detecting the position of a stock.

RULES FOR DETERMINING CULMINATION BY VOLUME OF SALES

Rule 1: At the end of any prolonged bull campaign or rapid advance in an individual stock, there is usually a large increase in the volume of sales, which marks the end of the campaign, at least temporarily. Then, after a sharp decline on heavy volume of sales, when a secondary rally takes place and the volume of sales decreases, it is an indication that the stock has made final top and that the main trend will turn down.

Rule 2: If the stock holds after making a second lower top and gets dull and narrow for some time, working in a sideways movement, and then breaks out on increased volume, it is a sign of a further decline.

Rule 3: After a prolonged decline of several weeks, several months, or several years, at the time a stock is reaching bottom, the volume of trading should decrease and the range in fluctuation should narrow down. This is one of the sure signs that liquidation is running its course and that stock is getting ready to show a change in trend.

Rule 4: After the first sharp advance (when the trend is changing from a bear market to a bull market) the stock will have a secondary reaction and make bottom, just the same as it had a secondary rally after the first sharp decline. If the volume of sales decreases on the reaction and then the stock moves up, advancing on heavier volume, it will be an indication of an advance to higher levels.

These rules apply to the general market, that is, to the total sales traded in on the New York Stock Exchange - daily, weekly or monthly - as well as to individual stocks.

Summary: Sales increase near the top and decrease near the bottom, except in abnormal markets like October and November 1929, when the market was moving down very fast and culminated on large volume of sales, making a sharp bottom, from which a swift rebound followed. As a rule, after the first sharp rally, there is a secondary decline on decreased volume, as described under Rule 4.

MONTHLY RECORD OF VOLUME OF SALES ON NEW YORK STOCK EXCHANGE
1929-1935

To understand the importance of Volume, a study of the total number of shares traded in on the New York Stock Exchange is necessary.

In July and August 1921, at the bottom of the Bear Campaign, the volume of sales was around 10,000,000 to 12,000,000 shares per month. In March 1928, sales reached 84,000,000 shared per month for the first time in history. After that, the volume of sales was very large, with this group of stocks working higher right along after the reaction in June 1928. The volume increased enormously in November 1928, reaching 114,000,000 shares, the largest for any month up to that time. Sales continued heavy in December 1928, and, in fact, right up to the top in 1929.

1929

September: Sales were over 100,000,000 shares. The Averages reached 386, the highest price in history.

October: For the first time since May 1929, the Averages broke under the low level of a previous month, which showed that the trend had turned down. All records for volume of sales were broken in October, sales reaching 141,000,000 shares.

November: At the bottom of a panicky decline in November, sales dropped down to 72,000,000 shares,

December: Sales 83,000,000 shares.

1930

January: Sales 62,000,000 shares.

February: 68,000,000 shares.

March: Volume of sales reached 96,000,000 shares.

April: Total volume reached 111,000,000 shares on a very small gain in price of the Averages.

May: In the early part of the month, the Averages broke under the April low, which was the first time that they had broken a monthly low since bottom was reached in November. Sales for May were 78,000,000 shares. A sharp decline followed.

June: Sales were 80,000,000 shares, with the market moving lower.

July & August: On a small rally, the total sales were only 80,000,000 for two months.

September: The market was slightly higher early in the month, then a decline started, which carried prices to new low levels, sales of 50,000,000 shares being recorded.

October: The market broke to new low levels. Stocks at this time broke the low levels of November 1929 and sales increased to 70,000,000 shares.

December: The Dow-Jones Industrial Averages declined 46 points under the low levels of November 1929. Total sales this month were 60,000,000 shares.

1931

January: A rally started and in January 1931 the sales were 42,000,000 shares.

February: The market made top of the rally on sales of 64,000,000 shares, which showed that the volume of trading was increasing on the rally and that stocks were meeting resistance. Note that this top was just under the low levels of November 1929, which showed that stocks met selling when they moved up under old low levels of the panic.

March: A decline started in March and the sales were 64,000,000 shares, a heavier volume, with prices moving lower.

April: Sales were 54,000,000 shares.

May: Sales 47,000,000.

June: There was a sharp decline on a volume of sales totaling 59,000,000, which carried the Averages down to new low levels, reaching 120, the old top of 1919 and the last low of May 1925. A quick rally followed to the end of June and early July, the Averages reaching 157½, but failing to cross the high level made in May 1931.

July: The sales were smaller, only 33,000,000, and the market narrowed down.

August: The sales were 24,000,000, still a narrow, dull market, not making much progress on the upside.

September: Activity started and sales reached 151,000,000. On this increased volume the Averages declined 45 points during the month of September. This showed great weakness and indicated a further decline.

October: A sharp decline occurred which carried the Averages down to 85 on sales of 48,000,000 shares.

November: A rally followed, culminating on November 9. The Averages reached 119½, back to the old top of 1919, to the last low of 1925, and to the bottom of a previous rally. Failing to penetrate these old bottoms and cross the previous top, the market showed weakness and indicated that the trend was still down. Sales in November were 37,000,000, the volume decreasing on the rally.

December: The Averages declined to a new low for the move, making 72 on sales of 50,000,000 shares, the largest since September 1931. This indicated that big liquidation was still going on.

1932

January: The Averages reached a low of 70 on sales of 44,000,000 shares for the month.

February: Rallied to 89¾ on sales of 31,000,000 shares.

March: The Averages made about the same high on sales of 30,000,000 shares. Then the market went dead on the rally, stocks narrowing down.

April: The Dow-Jones 30 Industrial Averages broke 70, the low of January, and declined to 55 on sales of 30,000,000 shares.

May: The Averages broke 53, the old low levels of the panic of 1907 and 1914, which indicated lower prices; then declined to 45 on sales of 23,000,000 shares.

June: The range between extreme high and extreme low averaged 10 points and the Averages reached a new low on sales of 23,000,000 shares.

July: On July 8, 1932, the extreme low was reached, with the Averages down to 40½. The volume was very small and the Averages and individual stocks moved in a very narrow trading range, indicating the last stages of a bear market. Late in the month the Averages crossed the high of June, which indicated that the trend was turning up. Sales were 23,000,000 shares. The range was about 13 points on Averages.

At the low in July the Averages were down 345 points from 1929 high. The volume of sales for the three months - May, June and July - aggregated only 69,000,000 shares, the smallest since 1923, in contrast to over 100,000,000 shares per month at the top in September 1929 and 141,000,000 in the month of October 1929. This indicated that after such a drastic decline, liquidation had run its course and the trend was changing. The market really had been sold to a standstill. Traders and investors sold out everything because they feared things were going to get worse. It was the same old story: a bull market begins in gloom and ends in glory. All of the indications were plain: The small volume of sales and narrow range of fluctuations indicated that the end had been reached and that a change in trend was certain.

During the latter part of July 1932, the advance started.

August: There was a sharp rally in August on sales of 83,000,000 shares, more than for the entire three months past. This was on short covering and wise investment buying.

September: Top of the rally was reached on sales of 67,000,000 shares, with the Averages up 40 points from the low of July 8. After this advance to September on a large volume, distribution took place and the trend turned down. (Note that the total volume from July 8 to the top in September was 168 million shares.) The Averages failed to go higher in the third month. At no time from April 1930 to July 1932 had the Averages or most of the individual stocks rallied over two months. Therefore, to show a change in trend to a prolonged bull market, they would have to advance three full months or more.

October: After September, stocks worked slowly down on a small volume of sales. In October the sales were 29,000,000.

November: Sales were 23,000,000.

December: Sales 23,000,000.

1933

January: Sales were 19,000,000 shares.

February: The whole country was in a state of panic. Banks were failing right and left. People were panic stricken and selling stocks and bonds regardless of price. There were business failures, and when President Roosevelt was inaugurated on March 4, he immediately acted and closed all the banks in the United States. This marked the end of the secondary decline and started a constructive movement.

The Dow-Jones Industrial Averages declined to 50 in February, which was 9 points higher than the low of July 1932. Sales were only 19,000,000 shares, the smallest volume of any time on over 10 years and the smallest volume for any one month since the top in September 1929, a sure sign of bottom.

March: A rally started on increased sales. The volume was 20,000,000 shares.

April: The United States went off the gold standard. This started a rapid advance in stocks and commodities. Sales on the New York Stock Exchange were 53,000,000 shares this month.

May: The advance continued and the volume of trading reached 104,000,000 shares:

June: The volume increased to 125,000,000.

July: The sales were 120,000,000.

From March low to July high 1933, the total number of shared traded on the New York Stock Exchange was 422,000,000 shares and the Averages at the top in July were up 60 points from the low of February 1933. Very few people keep records and study enough to understand what the enormous volume of 422,000,000 shares meant. This was the greatest volume of sales of any bull campaign in the history of the New York Stock Exchange. It was greater than the last advance in 1929.

(From the last low in May 1929 to September 1929, the Averages advanced 96 points and total sales on the New York Stock Exchange were 350,000,000 shares.)

It was one of the wildest buying waves in history. Commodities advanced by leaps and bounds. People bought stocks regardless of price. Just think about it: Sales of 350,000,000 in three months - May, June and July 1933 - equal to the volume from May 1929 to September 1929. The signs were plain that the volume was telling the story of a wave of inflation. Commodities and stocks had advanced so rapidly and everybody had bought on such thin margin that a wide-open break occurred in four days from July 18th to 21st, carrying the Dow-Jones Averages down 25 points to 85. Cotton and Wheat broke badly at the same time on heavy liquidation. At this time Dr. E. A. Crawford failed. He was involved in commodities, said to be the largest amount ever known.

August and September: After the sharp decline in July, a rally followed in August and September, which carried the Averages within two points of the July high, making a double top. The volume of sales on this second rally was smaller. In August the sales were 42,000,000 and in September 43,000,000 shares. In these two months, the volume was only two-thirds of the total volume for July 1933.

October: The Dow-Jones 30 Industrial Averages declined to 82½, the last low before the start of a long advance. Sales decreased to 39,000,000 and the market became very dull and narrow. A slow rally started from the October lows.

November: Sales were 33,000,000 shares.

December: Sales 35,000,000.

1934

January: The sales this month were 54,000,000.

February: Sales 57,000,000 shares, with the top in February only slightly above the high in January. The Averages failed to get over one point above the high of July 1933, making a double top. Sales of

111,000,000 shares in over two months and the third time at the same level was a signal of top. Individual stocks especially showed plainly by the large volume and the slow progress they were making in February that they were getting ready to start down. The trend turned down in the latter part of February.

March: Sales reached 30,000,000 shares.

April: There was a slight rally on 29,000,000 shares.

May: Prices were lower on 21,000.000 shares.

June: There was a small rally and the volume decreased to 16,000,000 shares for the month.

July: On July 26, 1934, stocks made bottom on sales of nearly 3,000,000 shares for the day, with the Dow-Jones Averages to 85, slightly above the low level of October 1933.
For the month of July 1934, total sales were only 21,000,000 shares. Individual stocks moved in a narrow trading range, which showed that bottom was being made and the foundation laid for another bull campaign. The fact that an extreme high was reached in July 1933 was an indication that you should watch for a change in trend in July 1934, according to my rule to watch for a change in trend one year, two years, or three years from any important top or bottom.

August: The market rallied 11 points on Averages; sales 16,000,000 shares.

September: The market reached within one point of the July low. Sales were down to 12,000,000 shares, a sure sign of bottom, being the smallest sales per month in many years.

October: The market rallied in October on a slightly increased volume of sales, 15,000,000 shares.

November: The sales increased to 21,000,000 shares.

December: Prices were higher; sales 23,000,000 shares for the month.

1935

January: There was increased activity on sales of 19,000,000 shares.

February: The market reached the top of the rally. Sales only 14,000,000 shares, which was a sign that there was not enough buying power to carry prices through.

March: There was a big decline, which was the last before the market advanced to new highs. Sales were 16,000,000 shares.

April: Increased activity shown and stocks started advancing. Volume of sales was 22,000,000 shares, which showed that a bull market was under way.

May: The Dow-Jones 30 Industrial Averages crossed the high levels of 1933 and the top of February 1934, on sales of 30,000,000 shares. Individual stocks showed increased volume and many of them moved up to new high levels.

June: The Averages crossed 120, which was above the last high of November 9, 1931, a sure indication of higher prices. The sales for June were 22,000,000 shares.

July: New highs were reached by individual stocks and the Averages. Sales for the month were 29,000,000 shares.

August: More new highs for individual stocks and new highs for the Industrial Averages. Sales reached 43,000,000 shares, the highest since January and February 1934.

September: The advance continued and sales were 35,000,000 shares.

October: The Dow-Jones 30 Industrial Averages advanced to 142. The total sales for the month were 46,000,000 shares.

November: Sales 57,000,000 shares, practically the same as February 1934 when stocks made top. The Averages reached 149 ½, up 109 points from the low of July 1932. During the week ended November 23, 1935, when the Averages reached top, the total volume of sales was nearly 19,000,000 shares, the largest since the week ended February 10, 1934, when top was reached. After such an enormous volume, with the Averages up 53 points since March 1935, according to my rule it was time to watch for top and a change in trend in stocks that had had big advances.

December: A reaction followed which carried the Averages down over 10 points from the November high. The volume of sales for the month was 45,000,000 shares.

JULY 1934 TO NOVEMBER 1935

The total sales from the low of July 26, 1934, to the high of November 20, 1935, were 407,000,000 shares. The total number of points which the Dow-Jones Industrial Averages advanced from July 1934 to November 20, 1935, was 65 points. Note that the total advance from the low of March 1933 to the top in July 1933 was 60 points. Therefore, with the Averages in November 1935 up 65 points, 5 points more than in the 1933 campaign, it was time to watch for at least a temporary change in trend.

Note that volume of sales during the 16 months' campaign from July 1934 to November 1935 was about 15,000,000 shares less than during the 5 months' campaign from March 1933 to July 1933. This shows that after the Securities Administration Law became effective, it reduced trading considerably.

If you continue to study the Volume of Sales on the New York Stock Exchange and watch the position of the Dow-Jones Industrial Averages, you will be able to detect culminations with greater accuracy.

CHAPTER VII

A PRACTICAL TRADING METHOD

To be profitable, a method for trading in the stock market must work in practice as well as in theory. Several years ago, I originated a practical trading method and since 1932 have made some important improvements which I have tested in my actual trading. I am giving my readers the benefit of this valuable discovery.

With this method you use the Weekly High and Low Chart, which is the best chart for trading purposes, but when stocks are very active and selling at very high levels, you can use the Daily Chart and apply the same rules to detect a change in trend, buying and selling levels, and points for stop loss orders.

I am giving the rules and making the trades on paper covering a period of more than 10 years to prove to you that big profits can be made by following these rules.

Rule 1 - Amount of Capital Required

To make speculation or investment a successful business, you must know the amount of capital required to begin trading and continue to trade. To be safe, I consider that at least $3,000 should be used for trading in each 100 shares of stock, and if you follow the rules you will make money. For trading in 10-share lots, a capital of $300 should be used.

Never risk more than 10% of your capital on any one trade. If you have as many as two or three losses, then reduce your unit of trading, using only 10% of your capital.

When profits have increased to the amount of your capital, say $3,000, then you can increase your trading unit to 200 shares, but after you have accumulated a large amount of profits, keep a larger amount of capital behind each trade.

Safety must be your first principle at all times. When large profits have accumulated, establish a reserve fund for protection, placing this money in a savings bank, first mortgages or gilt-edge investments for income.

Rule 2 - Always Use Stop Loss Orders

Never fail to place a stop loss order on each trade that you make, and let these stop loss orders be 1, 2, or 3 points away from the price at which you buy or sell, and under any conditions - even when stocks are at very high levels - on your first trade never risk more than 5 points or $500 on each 100 shares.

As a rule, a 3-point stop loss order is the safest to use, as it will be caught less than any other.

After a prolonged advance, when stocks are advancing very fast and at high levels, if you have big profits, then follow up with a stop loss order 5 points below the high price of each day, or 1 to 3 points under the low or closing price of the day. In case a stock is selling at very high levels, follow up with a stop loss order 10 points under the high price of each day.

When you make initial trades, never risk 10 points of your capital on any one trade. Five points must be the limit, and when it is possible, always try to make a trade where your risk is only 2 or 3 points.

Follow up profits with stop loss orders 1, 2, 3, or 5 points under each week's bottom on the long side, and follow down with a stop loss order 1, 2, 3, or 5 points above the top of each week on the short side.

Rule 3 - How to Detect Buying Points

Buy against double or triple bottoms and place a stop loss order 1, 2, or 3 points below them.

Buy when a stock holds 1, 2, 3 or more weeks around the same low level, and place a stop loss order 1, 2, and never more than 3 points under the lowest weekly bottom.

Buy when a stock crosses the previous high by 1 to 3 points. In most cases it is safer to wait until it had advanced 3 points above an old top before you decide that the trend has given a definite indication that it is going higher. Then, after it has crossed an old top by 3 points, it should not react 3 points under the old top. For example: If the old top is 50 and it advances to 53, then it should not react to 47 again. Therefore, On a reaction to around 51 to 48, you should buy and place stop loss order at 47, or 3 points under the old top.

When a stock advances into new high territory, that is, crosses the highest price of its history, it usually indicates higher prices and is safe to buy. If it is going higher the stock seldom reacts 3 points under the old high level.

Watch the tops of previous years. When a stock crosses the top of a previous year by 3 points, it is nearly always safe to buy, especially if it reacts back to the old top or slightly under it.

In a bull market, reactions only last 2 or 3 weeks before the main uptrend is resumed, therefore it is safe to buy at the end of two or three weeks' reaction after the stock shows that it is making bottom by holding 2 to 3 days.

Rule 4 - How to Detect Selling Points

Sell against double and triple tops and place a stop loss order 1, 2, or 3 points above them.

When old bottoms or low levels of previous movements are broken, sell short and place a stop loss order 1, 2, and never more than 3 points above the old bottom. It is always safest to wait until a stock breaks 3 points under an old bottom, then sell at the market or on a small rally and protect with a stop loss order 3 points above the old bottom.

Than, after stock has broken to new low levels, follow down your short position with stop loss order one point above the high of the previous

74

week and watch for a point where there is an old bottom or previous low level to cover shorts and buy again.

As a rule, a rally in a bear market only lasts two to three weeks; therefore, at the end of the second or third week, it is safe to go short with a stop loss order 3 points above the high of the previous week.

Watch the bottoms of previous years. When the stock breaks a bottom of a previous year by 3 points, it is nearly always safe to sell short, especially if it rallies up to the old bottom or slightly above it.

Rule 5 - How to Pyramid

It is important to know how and when to pyramid. When stocks are at low levels, between 20 and 50, you can buy or sell every 5 points apart if your capital and margin warrant it, that is, when you have 5 points' profit on the first trade, buy or sell an additional amount and place a stop loss order so that you will not have any loss on the two trades if the market should reverse and catch the stop.

When stocks are selling between 80 and 200 per share, you should only buy or sell 10 points apart. After you make the first commitment, then wait until you have 10 points' profit, then buy or sell a second lot. After you have bought or sold the fourth or fifth lot in a pyramid, then you should decrease the trading unit. For example:

If you have been buying 100 shares each 5 or 10 points up and have accumulated 500 shares, then it is safer to reduce your trading to 50 shares every 5 or 10 points up. If you have been trading in 200 shares and have bought 4 or 5 lots, then reduce your trading to 100-share lots. Reverse this rule on the short or selling side.

The big money is made by always following the main trend of a stock. Never buy a second or third lot unless the first trade has moved in your favor.

Never average a loss. To average a loss is the greatest mistake that any trader can make.

Rule 6 - When to Reverse Position

By reversing position, I mean that if you have been buying and pyramiding, then, when there is a change in trend and an indication to sell out long stocks, you should also sell short. For example:

If a stock advances to around 75, where there is an old top, and holds 1 or 2 weeks, you should sell out longs and go short and place a stop loss order at 78 or 3 points above the old low top. Then, if the stop at 78 is caught, you should cover shorts and go long again because you must keep with the trend all the time.

Apply the same rule when a stock is declining. When there is a change in trend and the time comes to cover shorts, then you should buy for long account again, just as I show in all the trades made in Chrysler Motors.

Rule 7 - Volume of Sales

By following the rules given in my books on Volume, you will be able to detect when tops and bottoms are reached and a change in trend takes place.

Nearly always when stocks are advancing rapidly and reach high levels, the Volume of sales increases. After the first quick, sharp reaction, there is a secondary rally, and if the main trend is going to turn down, the Volume will be smaller than it was on the advance when the final top was made. (See example of Volume on Chrysler at the end of this chapter)

After a prolonged decline, a decrease in Volume is an indication that liquidation has about run its course and a change in trend is due.

In panicky markets, when stocks have sharp declines, they often make bottom on large Volume and a rally follows on fair-sized Volume, then there is a secondary decline when Volume falls off considerably.

Look up the volume of each individual stock and judge its position according to the amount of stock outstanding. For example: General

76

Motors with 44,000,000 shares must move much slower and require more time to advance a point than Auburn Motors or J. I. Case which have such a small number of shares outstanding. Chrysler Motors has only 4½ million shares compared with 44,000,000 of General Motors, which is the reason Chrysler made a greater range between 1932 and 1935 than General Motors.

THE FOLLOWING OF RULES MAKES PROFITS

The human element beats most traders. The market does not beat them. Eliminate human judgment and guesswork. Do not buy or sell on hope or fear.

The man who will make up his mind to follow rules strictly to the letter will make profits. Prove to yourself that the rules work which I give you and then follow them. Buy or sell when the rules indicate that it is time to buy or sell, and then do no close trades and take profits until the rules indicate that it is time for a change in trend; then make your trades accordingly and you will make a success.

CHAPTER VIII

FUTURE OF STOCKS

FULFILLED PREDICTIONS

When I wrote THE TRUTH OF THE STOCK TAPE in 1923, I said that chemicals, airplanes and radio stocks would be the leaders in the next bull market. They did lead in the 1924-1929 Bull Campaign and these groups of stocks showed some of the greatest advances.

In the chapter on "Stocks of the Future" of page 191 of WALL STREET STOCK SELECTOR, which I finished in April 1930, I said that chemicals, radio stocks, airplane and moving picture stocks would be the leaders of the future bull campaign. This prediction has been fulfilled. Radio "B" sold at $3 per share in 1932 and advanced to $92 per share in December 1935. United Aircraft sold at 6½ in 1932 and later advanced to 46⅞. Allied Chemical sold at 42½ in 1932 and advanced to 173 in 1935. Air reduction sold at 30⅞ in 1932, then advanced to 171 in 1935. In this new book, I will show you how easy it was to detect these stocks that developed into early leaders and had big advances while others held in a narrow trading range, or declined during the bull market.

In Chapter IX, page 198 of WALL STREET STOCK SELECTOR, written in April 1930, I wrote as follows:

"The public learned about automobile stocks in 1915 and 1916, when they had their big advances, and then again in 1919. But from 1924 to 1929 the public bought automobile stocks on a scale greater than even before in any group of stocks. Therefore, the motors are greatly overbought and most of the companies are greatly overcapitalized. They have paid stock dividends and increased their stock to such an extent that they cannot pay dividends during the years of depression to come. Therefore, the automobile stocks will be among the best short sales in the coming bear market."

This prediction was amply fulfilled. Auburn Motors sold at 514 in 1929; 263¾ in April 1930 and 295½ in April 1931; declined to 15 in March and April 1935. Chrysler Motors which sold at 140½ in October 1928 and 43 in April 1930, declined to 5 in June 1932, a decline of 135½ points. General Motors, which had sold at a high of 54½ in April 1930, declined to 7⅝ in June 1932. Certainly, these declines were drastic enough to prove that I knew what I was talking about when I said in 1930 that motors were the best short sales.

On pages 203-204 of WALL STREET STOCK SELECTOR, I wrote as follows:

INVESTORS' PANIC

"About every 20 years there is an investors' panic or a severe depression, brought about by investors selling stocks at low levels. This is due to a prolonged decline and loss of confidence. Buying power having been reduced and investment selling continually coming into the market, force prices lower and lower, until banks call loans on high-class investment stocks, with the final result of a wide-open break or a sharp, severe decline. This occurred in 1837 to 1839, 1857, 1873, 1893, 1896, 1914, and 1920 to 1931. The panic of 1929 was not an investors' panic. It was a gamblers' panic.

"Various causes have produced these different panics, but the real basis behind all of them has been the money market. The banks, having become overloaded with loans during periods of prosperity, forced selling and produced the panic. Most bankers get too optimistic after a prolonged period of prosperity; then after a prolonged decline and business depression they become too pessimistic and are afraid to make loans. In fact, instead of making new loans, they call old loans, which makes the situation worse than it would be otherwise. It is the same with most of the newspapers. They know that it is popular to talk optimistic and they go to the extreme in good times and then when conditions get bad, they generally paint the picture blacker than it really is.

"Certainly, during all of these panics, some of the brokers and banks must have seen the handwriting on the wall and have known just exactly what was coming, but they never told their customers about it. Then the investor must *stop, look,* and *listen.* He must think for himself, and not depend upon his banker or his broker to get him out of the market at the right time, because past history proves that their advice at critical times cannot be depended upon.

"The coming investors' panic will be the greatest in history, because there are at least 15 to 25 million investors in the United States who hold stocks in the leading corporations, and when once they get scared, which they will after years of decline, then the selling will be so terrific that no buying power can withstand it. Stocks are so well distributed in the hands of the public that since the 1929 panic many people think that the market is panic-proof, but this seeming strength is really the weakest feature of the market. The public has never been good leaders and never will be, because their hopes and fears are easily excited. If stocks were all in the hands of a few strong men, then investors and the country would be safe, but when they are in the hands of millions of people who are unorganized and without leadership, then the situation is dangerous. A wise man will sell before it is too late. The public will hold on and hope; then all will become scared at the same time and sell when nobody wants to buy, the precipitating a panic. This was what caused the 1929 panic. The speculators and gamblers all got scared and sold at the same time.

"Greed and love of money will cause the next panic and the love of money will be the cause of the next war. 'War is hell!' You might ask what that has to do with stocks. War has always caused panics. War is coming and a panic is coming in stocks, and this time the panic in stocks may be the cause of the war. People often get a misconception of an idea or quote things wrong. We often hear people say, 'Money is the root of all evil.' In fact, the love of money and the quest for power has been the cause of all wars, as history proves. Love of money has been the cause of all financial troubles and depressions in the past, and the coming panic will be the greatest the world has ever known, because there is more money in the United States than ever before, therefore more to fight for. Men fight harder for money than anything else, once they see it slipping away."

80

It is a matter of record that the panic of 1931-1932 was the greatest in history with the most severe declines ever recorded in the history of the New York Stock Exchange. This prediction was based on my Master Time Factor, which enables me to tell months and years in advance when certain time cycles repeat and cause extreme high and low prices. This is enough to convince any man that my discoveries, based on mathematical science, can be depended upon to forecast future market movements.

HOW TRADERS AND INVESTORS WERE FOOLED IN 1930 TO 1932 PANIC

Investors and traders lost money in this great panic because they listened to other people who knew less about the market than they did and who were simply guessing. Many a so-called wise economist said that the bottom in November 1929 would not be broken and that this decline had corrected all the weak spots in the market and that the bull market would be resumed. They said the same thing about the breaks in 1930, 1931 and 1932. When the market actually reached bottom they did not know what to say because they had been fooled so long. They had not studied past history enough to know that after the greatest advance in history had culminated in 1929, the greatest panic in history must follow and that it would require a long time to liquidate stocks.

Every time stocks made bottom, the newspapers, government and economists said that it was the last bottom, but stocks went down, down, down until people lost faith in everything. They went lower than anybody dreamed they could go. This is what happens when everybody decided that stocks cannot go down or that stocks cannot go up - they always do the opposite. The public is always wrong, because they follow no well-defined rule and not organized. People believe that the government, by buying cotton, wheat and loaning money could the depression, but once a cycle is up and prices are due to decline, nothing can stop them until it has run its course. The same when the main trend turns up, neither government interferences nor anything else can stop the advance until it runs its course.

Every investor and trader should do his own studying and learn rules and apply them and not rely on other people who know no more about the market than he does.

HOW TRADERS AND INVESTORS MAY BE FOOLED IN THE FUTURE

During the year 1935, especially the last half of it, newspaper writers, statisticians and economists were all writing and talking about the abundance of cheap money and the large bank reserve. They talked about inflation and led people to believe that the government had changed conditions and money rates and that stocks must continue to go on up and up just because it is easy to get money. They forget the fact that this money, in many cases, is held by people who are too smart to buy stocks when they are too high.

Another fact that they have overlooked is that the money is not in liquid form. A large amount of money on deposit in the banks and held by insurance companies and saving banks is not in cash, but in government bonds, which if forced upon the market would break the bond market to pieces and result in a panic. When everybody is convinced an event is going to happen, it usually has already happened or has been discounted. People talk about inflation and how high stocks and commodities are going. My opinion is that we have had inflation ever since 1933 and that everything is discounted and that the market is getting ready to discount deflation before the election in the fall of 1936.

WHAT HAS HAPPENED TO CAUSE THE NEXT BEAR MARKET

The present administration at Washington with its New Deal, or I think it would be more proper to name it the "raw deal," decided to make it their business to run every other man's business, regardless of whether they knew anything about it or not. Most politicians and "brain-trusters" know nothing about running any kind of business. All they know or have is a theory on paper which will not work in practice. Their idea was to "crack-down" on business. If they could have had their way and General Johnson could have "cracked-down," as he tried to, on Henry Ford, his factory would have been closed and thousands of people would have been put out of business and men out of employment. The New Dealers assume the attitude that from him that hath it shall not be taken and given to him that hath not and does not work. Their policy is creating a nation of loafers. They area teaching people to depend upon the government and to depend upon other people who pay the taxes, which is the worst thing that could happen and must result in serious consequences sooner or later for the entire country. This country was developed by men who had the courage and the confidence to work from sun to sun. They were progressive and went into a new country and built up this country by work, and they can never build this country up by spending and not working. You cannot take the fruits of one man's labor and give it to another. You cannot tax one man who works and runs a successful business and give the money to other people who fail in business. It would be just as logical to tax one line of manufacturing business and give it to another business that is failing as it is to tax people who buy goods and give the money to farmers for ploughing up crops, destroying cattle and forcing the price so high that people who really work to pay for what they get, cannot afford to eat. The farmer can run his own business. He has always been able to run his business. If he cannot, then he will go down just as any other man who fails in business. It is a question of the old law of the survival of the fittest and the reward must go to those who work. No one has ever yet been able to get something good without paying for it. It cannot be done. We cannot beat the law of compensation. Nature pays off for work done, and the more work done, the more a man receives.

No one man or set of men is greater than all of the people of this country. The majority of the people voted to elect Roosevelt and did now know they were electing him to direct a lot of "brain-trusters" to run the country. Congress has submitted to Roosevelt and permitted "brain-trusters" to run things. The government is no different from any other business or individual who spends two or three times as much as it earns and may eventually go bankrupt. Government's interference with business and the government's heavy expenditures simply mean trouble ahead and a day of reckoning must come and the bill must be paid by the taxpayers, just the same as in the last panic which was the result of the World War and other foolish acts by our own government and foreign governments. We had to pay with the worst depression the world has ever seen. We cannot escape it in the future. It will cause another panic in stocks. When it comes, both traders and investors will sell stocks, as usual, after it is too late or in the last stages of the bear market, although stocks will decline on a smaller volume than in previous campaigns due to the restrictions of the Securities Exchange Law.

If the policies that are now being pursued in Washington continue for another four years, this county will be ruined. Banks that are loaded up with billions of bonds forced on them by the government will be unable to sell them to pay their depositors. Saving banks, insurance companies and trust companies loaded up with government bonds will find them depreciating 15 to 30 percent and then just suppose that government inflates and prints paper money, what will the money be worth? There is only one hope for this country and that is to stop this reckless spending and get down to business and work out of it. Governor Landon of Kansas had demonstrated that he can run the state government economically and has reduced the debt and is not spending more than they are taking in. This country will recover from the mistakes that have been made by the Roosevelt Administration if the spending is stopped and the budget is balanced. In future, instead of taxing business to death, businessmen should be allowed to run their own business to support legitimate expenditures of the government and not a nation of loafers.

Breinigsville, PA USA
09 February 2011
255193BV00002B/30/P